Strategies for Teaching
High School General Music

MENC wishes to thank
Carolynn A. Lindeman for developing and coordinating this series;
Keith P. Thompson and *Gloria J. Kiester*
for selecting, writing, and editing the strategies for this book;
and the following teachers for submitting strategies:

Stephan P. Barnicle
Judy Bond
J. Bryan Burton
Steven Calantropio
Jo-Ann L. Decker-St. Pierre
Michael Ellingsen
Wayne Feller
Barbara Geier
Jonathan Handman
Lloyd P. Hoover
Kathy Huselid
Colleen Tosi Ludeker
Larry McCaghy
Ellen McCullough-Brabson
Timothy Mahr
Brad Parkinson
Robert L. Peterson
Bruce Phelps
Melissa E. Popovich
Stephen Roemer
Victoria Smith
Jennifer Starr
Kathryn Troup
Valerie Vander Mark
Theo Rayburn Wee
William E. White
Chip Williams

Strategies for Teaching High School General Music

Edited by
Keith P. Thompson
and
Gloria J. Kiester

Published in partnership with
MENC: The National Association for Music Education
Frances S. Ponick, Executive Editor

Rowman & Littlefield Education
Lanham • New York • Toronto • Plymouth, UK

Published in partnership with
MENC: The National Association for Music Education

Published in the United States of America
by Rowman & Littlefield Education
A Division of Rowman & Littlefield Publishers, Inc.
A wholly owned subsidary of The Rowman & Littlefield Publishing Group, Inc.
4501 Forbes Boulevard, Suite 200, Lanham, Maryland 20706
www.rowmaneducation.com

Estover Road
Plymouth PL6 7PY
United Kingdom

First Rowman & Littlefield Education edition 2007
Copyright © 1997 by MENC: The National Association for Music Education

British Library Cataloguing in Publication Information Available

Library of Congress Control Number: 2007922710

ISBN-13: 978-1-56545-085-1 (pbk. : alk. paper)
ISBN-10: 1-56545-085-X (pbk. : alk. paper)

⊖™ The paper used in this publication meets the minimum requirements of
American National Standard for Information Sciences—Permanence of
Paper for Printed Library Materials, ANSI/NISO Z39.48-1992.
Manufactured in the United States of America.

CONTENTS

PREFACE

The Music Educators National Conference (MENC) created the *Strategies for Teaching* series to help preservice and in-service music educators implement the K–12 National Standards for Music Education and the MENC Prekindergarten Standards. To address the many components of the school music curriculum, each book in the series focuses on a specific curricular area and a particular level. The result is eleven books spanning the K–12 areas of band, chorus, general music, strings/orchestra, guitar, keyboard, and specialized ensembles. A prekindergarten book and a guide for college music methods classes complete the series.

The purpose of the series is to seize the opportunity presented by the landmark education legislation of 1994. With the passage of the Goals 2000: Educate America Act, the arts were established for the first time in our country's history as a core, challenging subject in which all students need to demonstrate competence. Voluntary academic standards were called for in all nine of the identified core subjects—standards specifying what students need to know and be able to do when they exit grades 4, 8, and 12.

In music, content and achievement standards were drafted by an MENC task force. They were examined and commented on by music teachers across the country, and the task force reviewed their comments and refined the standards. While all students in grades K–8 are expected to meet the achievement standards specified for those levels, two levels of achievement—proficient and advanced—are designated for students in grades 9–12. Students who elect music courses for one to two years beyond grade 8 are expected to perform at the proficient level. Students who elect music courses for three to four years beyond grade 8 are expected to perform at the advanced level.

The music standards, together with the dance, theatre, and visual arts standards, were presented in final form—*National Standards for Arts Education*—to the U.S. Secretary of Education in March 1994. Recognizing the importance of early childhood education, MENC went beyond the K–12 standards and established content and achievement standards for the prekindergarten level as well, which are included in MENC's *The School Music Program: A New Vision*.

Now the challenge at hand is to implement the standards at the state and local levels. Implementation may require schools to expand the resources necessary to achieve the standards as specified in MENC's *Opportunity-to-Learn Standards for Music Instruction: Grades PreK–12*. Teachers will need to examine their curricula to determine if they lead to achievement of the standards. For many, the standards reflect exactly what has always been included in the school music curriculum—they represent best practice. For others, the standards may call for some curricular expansion.

To assist in the implementation process, this series offers teaching strategies illustrating how the music standards can be put into action in the music classroom. The strategies themselves do not suggest a curriculum. That, of course, is the responsibility of school districts and individual teachers. The strategies, however, are designed to help in curriculum development, lesson planning, and assessment of music learning.

The teaching strategies are based on the content and achievement standards specified in the *National Standards for Arts Education* (K–12) and *The School Music Program: A New Vision* (PreK–12). Although the strategies, like the standards, are designed primarily for four-year-olds, fourth graders, eighth graders, and high school seniors, many may be developmentally appropriate for students in other grades. Each strategy, a lesson appropriate for a portion of a class session or a complete class session, includes an objective (a clear statement of what the student will be able to do), a list of necessary materials, a description of what prior student learning and experiences are expected, a set of procedures, and the indicators of success. A follow-up section identifies ways learning may be expanded.

The *Guide for Music Methods Classes* contains strategies appropriate for preservice instructional settings in choral, instrumental, and general music methods classes. The teaching strategies in this guide relate to the other books in the series and reflect a variety of teaching/learning styles.

Bringing a series of thirteen books from vision to reality in a little over a year's time required tremendous commitment from many, many music educators—not to mention the tireless help of the MENC publications staff. Literally hundreds of music teachers across the country answered the call to participate in this project, the largest such participation in an MENC publishing endeavor. The contributions of these teachers and the books' editors are proudly presented in the various publications.

—*Carolynn A. Lindeman*
Series Editor

---

*Carolynn A. Lindeman, professor of music at San Francisco State University and president of the Music Educators National Conference (1996–98), served on the MENC task force that developed the music education standards. She is the author of three college textbooks (*The Musical Classroom, PianoLab, *and* MusicLab) *and numerous articles.*

INTRODUCTION

Teaching general music in high school presents many challenges. Among these challenges is deciding just what general music in the high school is supposed to be. Within the context of this publication, high school general music refers to those courses and other music learning opportunities that are offered for students who elect not to participate in traditional high school ensembles. A high school general music course may be performance based as in the case of guitar, keyboard, handbell, or other instrumental classes; it may be listening based, similar to those courses labeled "music appreciation"; it may be an electronic music course that emphasizes the creation of new music; or it may be a potpourri of experiences with the art of music, similar to those provided in middle and elementary schools. Regardless of the label or packaging, high school general music in this publication consists of courses designed for students who for various reasons are not members of the band, orchestra, or chorus.

In a typical high school, the potential population for such courses would be approximately 85 percent of the student body. These students do not have lower intelligence or more negative attitudes than those in music ensembles. They do not lack musical talent or interest. If they are lacking in any way, it is in the genuine opportunity and motivation to become more actively involved in learning music. They may have been absent the day the band director came to the fourth grade to recruit young instrumentalists. They may not have been listening when the announcement was made about auditions for choir. They may have heard rumors that junior high band or choir was hard and decided not to continue their participation after elementary school, for fear that they would not be successful. They may have taken piano lessons for several years and discontinued them when the teacher moved. They may feel the strong need to fill their schedules with math, science, language, and other courses that they believe are essential for their future careers. For these and many other reasons, approximately 85 percent of the students in most high schools are not participating in performance ensembles.

The National Standards for Arts Education specify what every young American should know and be able to do in the arts. General music classes provide opportunities for every student to learn music at the elementary and middle school levels—we should feel compelled to provide comparable opportunities at the high school level. If the

National Standards for Music Education are to be met by every young American graduating from our high schools, formal instruction in music must be available for all students during the final years of schooling.

The goal of this publication is not to suggest course offerings or curriculum content, but rather to provide some examples of meaningful experiences through which that forgotten 85 percent of high school students can develop the skills and knowledge called for in the National Standards. Strategies are provided to serve as exemplars for each of the nine national standards. The depth and level of musical sophistication of these strategies vary greatly, as do the abilities of students in high school general music courses. If the National Standards are implemented consistently in general music courses at the elementary and middle school levels, students will enter high school general music courses with more uniform skills and knowledge in music. Until such time as the National Standards are fully implemented at the previous levels of schooling, great diversity must be expected in the musical ability of students in high school general music courses. This diversity is reflected in the strategies that follow.

Fortunately, general music at the high school level has gained the increasing attention of music educators and school administrators over the past ten years. While the number of high schools offering music courses for students not electing to participate in performance ensembles has increased significantly, general music courses are still a rarity in many high schools in this country. For that reason, many of the strategies presented in this publication have not been field tested with high school students. Many of the contributors indicated that they were planning courses for high school students and were delighted to share their ideas for learning activities. Others indicated a strong belief in the need for high school general music offerings and suggested ways that strategies that had been tested in middle or elementary schools might be adapted for older students.

Other books in this series contain ideas developed by masters in the field, writing about things they have done for years. This book is different in that the strategies suggested here have been developed by teachers with minimal experience in teaching general music in the high school. What these teachers have in abundance is faith, hope, imagination, and commitment.

Two principles guided the compilation of these strategies. These principles are important at all levels of learning, but are too frequently forgotten when working with older students:

1. Learning is most effective when students are actively involved in the learning process. Projects, performances, and small-group activities are preferred to teacher lecture or prolonged listening.

2. Learning music is most effective when students have quality aural experiences. Listening to and performing music is preferred to reading, talking about, or manipulating notational symbols.

The National Standards appropriately describe the skill and knowledge deemed necessary for being a musically informed citizen. Teachers must also recognize that it is important for students to develop a keen sense of the value that music adds to human life and that it is necessary for each student to develop the belief that he or she can be successful in musical endeavors. Without that belief and sense of value, there will be little motivation to learn.

The strategies that follow are not intended to provide a sequential outline or a course of study. They are a potpourri of activities intended to motivate the creative thinking of high school music teachers as they plan stimulating and meaningful opportunities in order for that forgotten 85 percent of the nation's high school students to gain essential music skills and knowledge—in order for those students to acquire "What every young American should know and be able to do in the arts."

STRATEGIES

Singing, alone and with others, a varied repertoire of music: Students sing music representing diverse genres and cultures, with expression appropriate for the work being performed. *

Objective

■ Students will sing accurately and with appropriate expression selected songs from the 1940s, describe the significance those songs had for people at that time, and compare the musical elements in those songs and current popular songs.

Materials

■ Copies of selected songs from the 1940s, such as "Don't Sit under the Apple Tree" (Miami: Warner Bros. Publications, 1942, 1954), also in *I'll Be Seeing You: Fifty Songs of World War II* (Milwaukee: Hal Leonard Corporation, 1995); "Sentimental Journey," in *I'll Be Seeing You: Fifty Songs of World War II*; "Aba Daba Honeymoon," from *Novelty Song Book* (Milwaukee: Hal Leonard Corporation, 1996); "Woody Woodpecker," from *TV Themes* (Milwaukee: Hal Leonard Corporation, 1994); "Comin' in on a Wing and a Prayer," from *Greatest American Song Book* (Milwaukee: Hal Leonard Corporation, 1996); "Deep in the Heart of Texas," in *The Music Connection,* Grade 6 (Parsippany, NJ: Silver Burdett Ginn, 1995) or

Procedures

1. As you accompany students on keyboard, have students sing several songs they know from the 1940s.

2. Ask several students to report on their interviews with senior citizens and share anecdotes about the songs the senior citizens remembered. Then have all students summarize their findings about the function of songs in the 1940s and the significance those songs had for people at that time.

3. Discuss with students the use of musical elements such as rhythm, melody, and timbre in the songs from the 1940s, and then have them make generalizations about modes, meters, rhythm patterns, and timbres in the songs of that era. Have students compare the use of musical elements in the songs from the 1940s with the use of musical elements in current popular songs. Discuss with students the possible reasons for the similarities and differences that they identify.

4. Help students select several songs from the 1940s to memorize. Then have students sing those songs, focusing on accuracy and expression and keeping in mind their interviews and the discussion of musical elements.

Indicators of Success

■ Students sing the 1940s' songs with accuracy and expression.

■ Students describe the significance of the 1940s' songs for people at that time.

■ Students describe the musical elements in the selected songs, comparing their use with the musical elements in current songs.

(continued)

---

* This is Standard 1C for Grades 5–8. Students at the 9–12 level are expected to demonstrate higher levels of the skills that are listed, deal with more complex music, and respond to music in increasingly more sophisticated ways. The strategy presented here illustrates how the standard that is listed could be put into action in grades 9–12.

World of Music, Grade 6
(Parsippany, NJ: Silver
Burdett Ginn, 1991); or
"Mairzy Doats" (Miami:
Warner Bros. Publications,
1943), also in *World of Music,*
Grade 3

Prior Knowledge and Experiences

- Students have sung selected songs from the 1940s.

- Students have listened to recordings by Bing Crosby, Frank Sinatra, Glenn Miller, and Benny Goodman.

- Students have interviewed senior citizens, using a questionnaire with questions such as the following: "What were your favorite songs in high school?" "What kinds of things did people sing about then?" "What purposes did music serve?" "Where did people sing?" "Describe the tunes, rhythms, and instruments used in music of that time."

Follow-up

- Take students on a field trip to a retirement center to join together with senior citizens in singing songs of the 1940s.

- Have students follow the same procedure to study the music of other groups, such as Latin Americans, Native Americans, or Vietnam War protesters.

Singing, alone and with others, a varied repertoire of music: Students sing music representing diverse genres and cultures, with expression appropriate for the work being performed. *

Objective

- Students will sing with expression and technical accuracy a Navajo song, identifying its musical characteristics and describing its cultural significance.

Materials

- "Jo'ashila," with directions for two-step dance and accompanying recording, in *Roots and Branches: A Legacy of Multicultural Music for Children*, by Patricia Shehan Campbell, Ellen McCullough-Brabson, and Judith Cook Tucker (Danbury, CT: World Music Press, 1994)
- Audio-playback equipment

Prior Knowledge and Experiences

- Students have sung songs from a variety of cultures and have examined the significance of the cultural context and the music.

Procedures

1. Ask students to listen to the Navajo song "Jo'ashila," and discuss with them the English translation of the text. Point out that while most words of the song are translatable, some are vocables (words that are integral to the meaning of the text but have no translation).

2. Have students listen to the song again, this time noticing the prominent features of the melody and the rhythm. Note the emphasis of the tonic note, the prominent outline of the triad, and the constant beat of the drum. After they discuss the structure of the piece, have students chant the words in rhythm.

3. Tell students to listen to the song again, this time for the tone color of the singer's voice. Have them describe this tone color and compare it to the tone color of other singers they have heard.

4. Ask students to keep all the things they have discussed in mind and to "think" the words and melody as you play the recording. Then ask students to sing the song with the recording.

5. Discuss the importance of the cultural context and music for "Jo'ashila." Explain that it is a traditional Navajo social song that may be performed as part of the Enemy Way Ceremony, a three-day ritual used to purify Navajos who are exposed to "outsiders." In addition, the song may be performed at the Navajo Song and Dance Contest, a social event derived from the Enemy Way Ceremony.

6. Demonstrate the traditional two-step dance to the recorded accompaniment of "Jo'ashila." Then ask students to perform the dance with you.

7. Have students sing "Jo'ashila" as they do the two-step dance, thinking about the Navajos' reasons for singing this song.

(continued)

---

* This is Standard 1C for Grades 5–8. Students at the 9–12 level are expected to demonstrate higher levels of the skills that are listed, deal with more complex music, and respond to music in increasingly more sophisticated ways. The strategy presented here illustrates how the standard that is listed could be put into action in grades 9–12.

Indicators of Success

- Students sing "Jo'ashila" expressively and with technical accuracy.

- Students perform the traditional two-step dance.

- Students describe the musical characteristics of "Jo'ashila" and the significance of the performance of the song and the dance in their cultural context.

Follow-up

- Have students learn to perform songs of other Native American nations and of other cultures.

STANDARD 1C

Singing, alone and with others, a varied repertoire of music:
Students demonstrate well-developed ensemble skills.

Objective

- Students will sing a folk song in four parts, performing proper entrances and releases and singing phrases expressively.

Materials

- Choral octavo "Gentle Annie," by Stephen Foster, arr. Dennis Elliot, with accompanying recording, BP 113 (Columbus, OH: Beckenhorst Press), SATB

- Audiocassette recorder, microphone, and blank tape

Prior Knowledge and Experiences

- Students can read music.
- Students have listened to several Stephen Foster songs.

Procedures

1. Distribute the choral octavo "Gentle Annie" and familiarize the students with the octavo format. Ask students to follow the score as you play the recording of "Gentle Annie." After they have heard the recording, have students describe the mood the song communicates.

2. Help students to sing the song in parts by rote and sightreading. Have them find interpretive markings and describe how those markings should be expressed in their singing.

3. Discuss with students the importance of singing together and of factors such as entrances and releases that can make singing together more effective. Then have them practice entrances and releases until they are precise.

4. Have students listen as you demonstrate how to shape a phrase from "Gentle Annie." Ask them to apply the same technique to that phrase and to others in the song. After they have sung several phrases, ask students to describe the feelings conveyed by the melodic line. Have students try singing the last phrase with an ascending melody (that is, *do, re, mi, fa, sol, sol, sol, la, ti, do*); then have them compare the differences in the feeling between the descending and the ascending melodies. Remind students of the melodic lines in other pieces of music as part of a discussion about how composers use melodic line to communicate feelings such as joy, sorrow, or triumph.

5. Have students sing "Gentle Annie" expressively, giving attention to proper entrances, releases, and interpretive markings, and to the shaping of phrases.

6. Record students singing the song and have them critique their performance.

Indicators of Success

- Students perform proper entrances and releases in their singing of "Gentle Annie" as an ensemble.

- Students sing phrases of the song expressively.

(continued)

Follow-up

- Have students continue learning to sing "Gentle Annie," having them describe its musical elements and memorize it.

- Discuss with students the value of a song such as "Gentle Annie" to society. Ask them to define "emotional literacy" and describe how it contributes to the development of the fully human person.

- Have students apply the skills and understandings they learned with "Gentle Annie" to other Stephen Foster songs.

Singing, alone and with others, a varied repertoire of music:
Students demonstrate well-developed ensemble skills.

Objective

- At an assembly to observe Martin Luther King Day, students will sing African American spirituals and songs of the Civil Rights Movement with a uniform sound, blending their voices well together and singing their parts accurately and expressively.

Materials

- "When the Saints Go Marching In," in *The Music Connection,* Grade 8 (Parsippany, NJ: Silver Burdett Ginn, 1995); *Share the Music,* Grade 5 (New York: Macmillan/McGraw-Hill, 1995); *Music and You,* Grade 5 (New York: Macmillan/McGraw-Hill, 1991); or *World of Music,* Grade 8 (Parsippany, NJ: Silver Burdett Ginn, 1991)

- "Oh, Freedom," in *The Music Connection,* Grade 8

- "Lift Ev'ry Voice and Sing," in *The Music Connection,* Grade 8; *Share the Music,* Grade 5; *Music and You,* Grade 6; or *World of Music,* Grade 8

- "Free at Last," in *The Music Connection,* Grade 8, or *Share the Music,* Grade 5

Procedures

1. Give a brief welcome to students at the assembly. Ask students to stand and sing "When the Saints Go Marching In," with choir sopranos singing a descant. Encourage a vigorous tempo, expressive singing, and good vocal technique.

2. Without pause, have accompanist play an introduction to "Oh, Freedom," direct the choir to begin to sing, and then have everyone join in. On the repeat, encourage students to harmonize and to sing with a uniform sound, giving attention to blending their voices well. Have a soloist sing a descant on the final stanza.

3. Remind the students that James Weldon Johnson and J. Rosamond Johnson, who wrote "Lift Ev'ry Voice and Sing," were distinguished African Americans known for their contributions to music, law, diplomacy, literature, and civil rights. Then have everyone sing this song, holding each note to its full value and building to a crescendo in the third and seventh phrases, and executing entrances and releases together.

4. Have a student read Martin Luther King's "I Have a Dream" address.

5. Without pause, direct choirs to begin singing "Free at Last." Have soloists sing the verses, and let everyone join in on the chorus and the responses. Encourage jubilant, rhythmic, ensemble singing.

6. Remind students that Marian Anderson, an African American and one of the great contraltos of the twentieth century, was once shut out from performing on an American operatic stage. She then went to Europe where she established a brilliant operatic career. At home she was subject to many indignities because of her race. When Anderson was denied access to Constitution Hall to sing, Eleanor Roosevelt arranged for her to sing on the steps of the Lincoln Memorial. More than 75,000 people came, and she opened her program with "My country 'tis of thee, Sweet land of liberty, Of thee I sing. . . . " Her profound contributions toward racial harmony were later continued in the work of Martin Luther King. Ask students to try to imagine Anderson's thoughts as they sing "America."

(continued)

- "America," in *Share the Music,* Grade 6; *Music and You,* Grade 8; or *World of Music,* Grade 8

- "We Shall Overcome," in *The Music Connection,* Grade 8; *Music and You,* Grade 4; or *World of Music,* Grade 8

- "I Have a Dream," Martin Luther King address, in *Let the Trumpet Sound: The Life of Martin Luther King, Jr.* by Stephen B. Oates (New York: HarperCollins, 1994)

Prior Knowledge and Experiences

- Students have participated in assembly singing in elementary, middle, and high school.

- In general music classes, students have learned to sing the selected songs with good vocal technique and from memory.

- Students have been asked to evaluate their ensemble skills at the assembly and to be prepared to make suggestions for improved singing when they meet in class later.

- Students in choirs have prepared special parts.

- In social studies, students have participated in discussions about the significance of Martin Luther King Day.

7. Close the assembly by asking everyone to stand and sing "We Shall Overcome." Encourage students to harmonize and to listen to each other for balance, blending their voices to achieve a uniform sound.

Indicators of Success

- Students sing with a uniform sound, blending their voices well together.

- Students sing with expression, technical accuracy, and enthusiasm.

- Students request opportunities to sing the songs in class, and they continue to sing them in informal situations.

Follow-up

- Have students evaluate their ensemble skills and the expressiveness and accuracy of their singing at the assembly and make suggestions for improvement. Ask them to discuss the range of emotions expressed in the songs and the possible effects these songs have had on people involved in the Civil Rights Movement.

- Have students apply their knowledge and skills to new songs, singing them expressively and accurately.

- Have students investigate other times when songs have played a significant role, such as during the period of the Vietnam War. Help them to develop a repertoire of songs from that time.

STANDARD 1C

STRATEGY 3 OF 3

Singing, alone and with others, a varied repertoire of music:
Students demonstrate well-developed ensemble skills.

Objective

- Students will sing in small and large groups expressively and with a uniform sound both the karaoke and the printed arrangements of a song.

Materials

- Karaoke CD and sheet music for a popular song
- Recording of the selected popular song
- Karaoke system with television monitor
- Audio-playback equipment
- Audiocassette recorder, microphone, and blank tape
- Performance evaluation sheets

Prior Knowledge and Experiences

- Students have studied music theory.
- Students can follow piano and vocal scores.
- Students have discussed the art of song arranging.
- Students have prepared an evaluation sheet for rating their singing performance.
- Students are familiar with the selected popular song.

Procedures

1. Demonstrate for students how the karaoke system with television monitor works. Explain that this kind of singing originated in Japan and that business and professional associates there often dine together and then sing for each other. Westerners who do business in Japan are frequently at an advantage if they are comfortable singing.

2. Review with students their discussion of the art of song arranging.

3. Ask students to examine the score of the selected popular song, sing the song together with keyboard accompaniment, and identify its musical features (for example, dynamics and tempo markings).

4. Have students listen to the recording and note the differences between the recording and the printed score by circling the appropriate places on the score as they listen. Discuss with the students what those differences are.

5. Have students sing the song together from the printed score. Then ask students to sing it in small groups, concentrating on listening to each other and achieving a uniform sound. Also, have them give attention to executing dynamics and tempo or other expressive markings uniformly to improve their ability to sing as an ensemble. Encourage the listeners to offer suggestions for improving the performance.

6. Have students listen to the karaoke arrangement of the song and then sing it in small groups using the karaoke system. Ask students which version of the song they prefer and why.

7. Distribute the performance evaluation sheets and discuss the components of a good singing performance, with particular attention to ensemble skills. Record the class as they perform the version that most students prefer. Then play the tape for the class and have each student use the evaluation sheet to rate the class performance. Discuss the evaluations.

(continued)

Indicators of Success

- Students identify the musical differences in the printed and karaoke arrangements of the song.

- Students demonstrate good ensemble skills, including singing with a uniform sound and executing expressive markings uniformly.

- Students sing the song with expression and technical accuracy.

Follow-up

- Have students sing other songs with the karaoke system and continue to improve their ensemble skills.

- Have students sing individually with the karaoke system, giving them the opportunity to improve their singing technique and confidence level.

Advanced

STANDARD 1D

Singing, alone and with others, a varied repertoire of music: Students sing with expression and technical accuracy a large and varied repertoire of vocal literature with a level of difficulty of 5, on a scale of 1 to 6.

Objective

- Students will sing a four-part choral arrangement of a Newfoundland folk song with a level of difficulty of 5, demonstrating accurate rhythms and appropriate dynamic contrasts.

Materials

- "Feller from Fortune," in *Elmer Iseler Choral Series,* arr. Harry Somers (Ft. Lauderdale, FL: Walton Music Corporation), SATB, Level 5

Prior Knowledge and Experiences

- Students have experience as choral singers, including having the ability to sing in parts and to sing melodic lines independent of other voices.

- Students have a well-developed understanding of rhythm.

- Students can identify musical terms and expressive markings.

Procedures

1. Have students read the text of "Feller from Fortune," identify its origin, and describe how they expect the piece to sound.

2. Ask students to note the various meters (7/8, 3/8, 6/8, 2/4, 9/8, 4/4, 5/8, 3/4), and discuss with them how they can move from one meter to another. Then have students tap eighth notes on their desks as they chant the text to the rhythm, keeping the eighth note constant throughout.

3. Have students tap an eighth-note rhythm on their desks and speak the soprano part, then the alto part, then the tenor part, and finally the bass part, working on any trouble spots. Ask them to note how the parts relate to each other and to describe the similarities and differences between them. For example, at the bottom of page 4, last measure, have students note how, initially, the sopranos and altos have the theme two measures apart while the basses and tenors provide rhythmic and tonal bass; at the top of page 5, all come together rhythmically to finish the verse. By keeping the eighth notes steady, the students can easily move from one meter to another.

4. Divide students into SATB sections and have them speak their respective parts at the same time, focusing on rhythmic accuracy. Tap a steady eighth-note rhythm as students speak their parts.

5. Have all students sing each part—soprano, then alto, then tenor, then bass—in their own range. (Depending on the students' sightreading ability, you may want to play the parts through once or twice before playing the accompaniment.) Repeat, having students observe the dynamic markings.

6. Have students sing their respective parts in the music at the same time at a slow tempo, focusing on rhythm and expressive markings.

7. Conclude by having students sing the song at a faster tempo.

(continued)

Indicators of Success

- Students sing their parts in "Feller from Fortune" with accurate rhythms and appropriate dynamic contrasts.
- Students execute meter changes while keeping a steady beat.

Follow-up

- Continue working on "Feller from Fortune," concentrating on trouble spots. Have students determine the proper phrasing and sing the song, focusing on phrasing as well as accurate rhythms and dynamic contrasts. Then have students focus on clean articulation, striving to sing the song at the given tempo and with good articulation.

STANDARD 1E

Singing, alone and with others, a varied repertoire of music:
Students sing music written in more than four parts.

Objective

- Students will sing a six-part canon with three ostinatos.

Materials

- "Summer Is A-Comin' In," with accompanying CD, in *Music and You,* Grade 6 (New York: Macmillan/McGraw-Hill, 1991)
- CD player
- Audiocassette recorder, microphone, and blank tape

Prior Knowledge and Experiences

- Students have studied Gregorian chant, troubadour songs, and early instrumental music and compared them with examples of contemporary instrumental music, contemporary love songs, and contemporary church and temple liturgies.

Procedures

1. Ask students to examine the thirteenth-century manuscript of "Summer Is A-Comin' In" in their texts and to try to read and sing the song. Have them compare this ancient notation with the modern notation in their text and describe the major differences between the two notation systems (for example, clef signs are different, notes do not have stems). Then have students chant the rhythm on "doo," using the modern notation.

2. Ask students to listen and follow the modern notation and text as you play the recording of the song. After they have listened to the recording, ask them to describe what they think the words mean.

3. Play the recording again, having students listen for any repeated rhythmic or melodic patterns. After listening, also ask students to describe the form of the song (a canon) and the relationship between the text and the melody, noting the way the word "cuckoo" is expressed in the melody.

4. Have students try singing the song. Help them to identify and correct performance problems until they can sing the piece in unison easily.

5. Teach the entire class all three ostinatos (measures 9–10, "Sing cuckoo"; measures 19–20, "cuckoo, cuckoo"; and measures 5–8, "Groweth seed and bloweth mead and springeth wood anew"). Assign each ostinato to a small group of students. Have students sing the song through three times, each time adding an ostinato.

6. When students can sing the piece comfortably with all three ostinatos, have them sing it as a canon in two parts. Add additional parts at the distance of two or four measures, according to phrase lengths, each time students sing the song through, until the class is singing the canon in six parts with three ostinatos. Assist with keyboard, if necessary.

7. Record the students singing. Then play the tape and have students evaluate their singing, make corrections, and then sing the song again.

(continued)

Indicators of Success

- Students sing the song with technical accuracy and expression as a six-part canon with all three ostinatos.

- Students describe the differences between the thirteenth-century notation and the modern notation of the song.

Follow-up

- Ask students to speculate why "Summer Is A-Comin' In" has value and has survived for hundreds of years. Emphasize that music captures the emotions in a unique way and that it bridges the centuries, enabling people from different eras to share their feelings.

- Have students perform "Summer Is A-Comin' In" with one or two students on a part for English and social studies classes, when appropriate, as an example of music that is at least seven hundred years old. Also, have them perform other ancient music they have researched and share recordings of the oldest music they can find of particular ethnic groups.

STANDARD 1F

Singing, alone and with others, a varied repertoire of music:
Students sing in small ensembles with one student on a part.

Objective

- Students will sing a four-part round successfully with one student on a part, critiquing their vocal technique and musical accuracy.

Materials

- *Successful Warm-ups,* Book 1, by Nancy Telfer (San Diego: Neil A. Kjos Music Company, 1995)
- "Let Us Sing Together," in *Adventures in Singing* by Clifton Ware (New York: Glencoe/McGraw-Hill, 1995)

Prior Knowledge and Experiences

- Students have studied music theory.
- Students can sing melodic lines independent of other voices.

Procedures

1. Have students do several minutes of physical warm-ups, including stretching the upper part of the body. Explain that they are preparing for the muscular activity of singing. Then ask students to do the series of vocal warm-ups on page 25 of *Successful Warm-ups.*

2. Help students sing "Let Us Sing Together" one phrase at a time. Make sure they are secure in singing each phrase before learning the next one. (*Note:* If the pitches are uncomfortable for the students to sing, use another key.) When students have learned all the phrases, have them sing the entire song.

3. Discuss with students any problems they had in singing the song and help them identify how they can correct them. Have students sing the song again.

4. Ask students to describe ways to improve their singing by applying what they did in warm-ups (for example, focusing on correct posture and breath control). Have students sing the song again, using those ideas to improve their singing.

5. Have students sing the song first as a two-part round, then as a three-part round, and finally as a four-part round. Use the keyboard for assistance if necessary.

6. Ask small groups of students to sing the round in four parts with two voices to a part. Have other students evaluate their vocal technique (including posture, breath control, tone production, intonation, and phrasing) and technical accuracy (including correct pitch, rhythm, tempo, and dynamics). Discuss the evaluations of the small groups.

7. Have quartets of students sing the round in four parts.

Indicators of Success

- Students sing the four-part round successfully with one voice per part.
- Students critique their vocal technique and musical accuracy and improve their performances based on the critiques.

(continued)

Follow-up

- Have students work on a four-part choral piece in small groups, gradually building their skill until they can sing the piece with one voice on a part.

STANDARD 1F

Singing, alone and with others, a varied repertoire of music:
Students sing in small ensembles with one student on a part.

Objective

- Students will sing a three-part song as a class and in small ensembles with one student on a part.

Materials

- "Yonder Come Day," arr. Judith Cook Tucker (Danbury, CT: World Music Press), 2 or 3 parts

Prior Knowledge and Experiences

- Students can sing melodic lines independent of other voices.

Procedures

1. Tell students to step-clap, stepping on beats one and three and clapping on beats two and four in 4/4 meter. Then ask them to sing part 1 of "Yonder Come Day" while they continue stepping and clapping.

2. Have all students sing part 2 and then all sing part 3 while they step and clap.

3. Ask students to count off by threes, and then assign each number a part to perform. Have students sing the song with all three parts. Alternate parts so that each student sings each of the three parts at some time.

4. Have students sing the piece with two or three students on each part. Ask everyone to continue stepping and clapping as the ensemble performs.

5. Finally, have small groups sing the song with one student on each part as the rest of the class steps and claps. (If students are reluctant to sing, let them choose a backup singer or have other students in the class hum along.) Give every student the opportunity to sing alone on a part.

Indicators of Success

- Students sing "Yonder Come Day" in three parts in small ensembles.
- Students sing the song with one student on a part.

Follow-up

- Have students perform "Yonder Come Day" from memory.
- Have students learn to sing "Betelehemu" by Wendell Whalum, (New York: Lawson-Gould Music Publishers), SATB, with one student on a part.

Performing on instruments, alone and with others, a varied repertoire of music: Students perform on at least one instrument accurately and independently, alone and in small and large ensembles, with good posture, good playing position, and good breath, bow, or stick control. *

Objective

- Students will play a song on the guitar at a moderate tempo and with expression, with accurate right-hand fingering alternation and with left-hand fingering in the first position on the guitar.

Materials

- "Ode to Joy," in *Hal Leonard Guitar Method,* Book 1, by Will Schmid (Milwaukee: Hal Leonard Corporation, 1986)
- Guitars (one or two students per guitar)

Prior Knowledge and Experiences

- Students have been introduced to exercises 1–17 in the *Hal Leonard Guitar Method,* Book 1.

Procedures

1. Have students work in pairs, so that they can take turns acting as performer and coach, and practice warm-up exercises three times, alternating *im* (index, middle fingers), *ma* (middle, ring fingers), and *ia* (index, ring fingers).

2. As a preparation for learning "Ode to Joy," have students do an open-string warm-up, playing the strings in order one at a time in 4/4 meter at a moderate tempo, one note per beat: 1-2-3-4-5-6-5-4-3-2-1. Have them play this exercise as expressively as possible.

3. Have students sing the letter names for "Ode to Joy" and finger the notes with the left hand only. Then have them practice the piece using both hands, with the *im* right-hand fingering alternation. Ask coaches to monitor the fingering of both hands. Make sure that all students have the opportunity to practice the piece on the guitar.

4. Have students play "Ode to Joy" as a group while coaches continue to monitor playing technique. Then switch the performers and coaches and repeat the song.

5. Have half of the class perform as the other half evaluates the accuracy and expressiveness of the playing and makes suggestions for improvement. Again, switch performers and coaches and repeat the performance and evaluation so that all students have the opportunity to play and to evaluate.

6. Have students implement suggestions for improvement and perform "Ode to Joy" as a class. Then ask individual students to perform for the class.

Indicators of Success

- Students play "Ode to Joy" at a moderate tempo with accurate right-hand fingering alternation and with accurate left-hand fingering in the first position.
- Students play expressively.

---

* This is Standard 2A for Grades 5–8. Students at the 9–12 level are expected to demonstrate higher levels of the skills that are listed, deal with more complex music, and respond to music in increasingly more sophisticated ways. The strategy presented here illustrates how the standard that is listed could be put into action in grades 9–12.

Follow-up

■ Have students listen to "Ode to Joy," the first portion of Ludwig van Beethoven's Symphony no. 9, fourth movement, and discuss what they think Beethoven was trying to communicate, what orchestral means he used to communicate his message, and why this music is considered such a masterpiece.

Performing on instruments, alone and with others, a varied repertoire of music: Students perform on at least one instrument accurately and independently, alone and in small and large ensembles, with good posture, good playing position, and good breath, bow, or stick control. *

Objective

- Students will play a five-finger piece on the keyboard with technical accuracy and expression.

Materials

- First piece in *The First Term at the Piano* by Béla Bartók (New York: Editio Musica Budapest/Boosey & Hawkes, 1929); also called "Study," in *Group Piano for Adults,* Book 1, by E. L. Lancaster and Kenon D. Renfrow (Van Nuys, CA: Alfred Publishing Company, 1995) or "Unison Melody," in *PianoLab: An Introduction to Class Piano,* 3rd ed., by Carolynn A. Lindeman (Belmont, CA: Wadsworth Publishing Company, 1996)
- Keyboards (one per student)

Prior Knowledge and Experiences

- Students have studied music theory.
- Students can identify the notes on the Grand Staff by letter name and can play simple melodic patterns on the keyboard.

Procedures

1. Have students practice playing whole steps and half steps on their keyboards by asking them to play certain pitches and then to play each pitch a step or a half step up or down. For example, tell them, "D up a step" or "G down a half step."

2. Explain to students that for the next exercise, the thumb would be number 1, and so on. Then ask students to place right-hand fingers on the keyboard and play a given pitch with the thumb (1) and then a fifth above with the little finger (5); for example, D and A. Have them do the same with the left hand (little finger is 1, thumb is 5).

3. Have students play five-finger patterns (the first five pitches of an ascending major scale) in a steady rhythmic pattern. Ask them to repeat this without looking down at their hands. Then ask students to repeat the five-finger patterns, followed by the 1-3-5 pitches in that pattern played simultaneously (a triad in block-chord form). Repeat this step with the other hand.

4. Have students read the rhythm of the Bartók piece by calling each quarter note "one," and each half note "one-two"; for example, "one-one-one-one one-two-one-one one-two-one-two," and so on. Remind students to accent the strong beats. Then have them play the pitches of the treble and bass parts separately in rhythm.

5. Look at the expressive markings with the students and help them decide how to apply those in the music. Ask them to play the pitches of each part again with accurate rhythm, observing the expressive markings.

6. Have students play both parts together. Ask them to evaluate the accuracy and expressiveness of their own playing.

7. Have students apply the suggestions from their self-evaluations and take turns playing the piece in small groups for the class.

---

* This is Standard 2A for Grades 5–8. Students at the 9–12 level are expected to demonstrate higher levels of the skills that are listed, deal with more complex music, and respond to music in increasingly more sophisticated ways. The strategy presented here illustrates how the standard that is listed could be put into action in grades 9–12.

Indicators of Success

■ Students play the Bartók piece on the keyboard with technical accuracy and expression.

Follow-up

■ Have students learn to play "March," by Daniel Gottlob Türk, and "Bright Lights Boogie," by Gayle Kowalchyk and E. L. Lancaster, in *Group Piano for Adults,* Book 1, emphasizing appropriate tempo and dynamics and sensitive phrasing. Have them also compare the use of inflection, accents, and pacing in effective and ineffective spoken language (speaking: "It was a dark and stormy night") with the use of expression in effective musical communication.

STANDARD 2A

Performing on instruments, alone and with others, a varied repertoire of music:
Students perform with expression and technical accuracy a large and varied repertoire
of instrumental literature with a level of difficulty of 4, on a scale of 1 to 6.

Objective

- Students will play handbells with expression and technical accuracy as they perform a Level 4 piece, demonstrating the solo handbell techniques of cross-over and weave.

Materials

- "My Savior's Love: Medley with 'And Can It Be' and 'I Stand Amazed in the Presence'," arr. Christine Anderson (Nashville: Word/Nelson Music)
- Handbells A4 to B♭6
- Handbell tables with pads

Prior Knowledge and Experiences

- Students have studied music theory.
- Students have studied basic handbell technique.
- Students have been introduced to cross-overs, R and L, and weave.

Procedures

1. Lay the bells out in keyboard order, with these exceptions: Place A4 between E♭5 and F#5; place E♭6 after B♭6. Explain the order of the bells to the students, noting that the bells are normally laid out in keyboard order, but exceptions are made here to facilitate playing.
2. Review the cross-over technique with sudents. Then have them practice the cross-over at measures 13, 30, and 31 in "My Savior's Love: Medley."
3. Review the meaning of R and L. Then ask students to change measure 25 from R-L to L and to play R-L in measure 26. Review the weave technique and have students practice weave at measures 25–26 and at measures 28, 32, and 59.
4. Have students play measures 65–72 in the upper octave for effect. (*Note:* This change to the upper octave enhances the melody, creating a more interesting result than continuing to play in the lower octave.)
5. Have students practice the piece until they achieve facility in ringing the bells. Then have them evaluate the accuracy of their playing and make any necessary corrections.
6. After students correct technical errors and play the piece again, ask them to evaluate the expressiveness of their playing and suggest ways to make it more expressive. Have them play the piece a final time, concentrating on both technical accuracy and expression.

Indicators of Success

- Using cross-over and weave techniques, students perform "My Savior's Love: Medley" on handbells with accuracy and expression.

Follow-up

- Have students memorize the music for "My Savior's Love: Medley," for ease of performance and more focus on expressive playing.
- To help students gain greater facility in using the cross-over and weave techniques, introduce other music using these techniques.
- Have students learn more difficult techniques, including "shelley" and "table damping." Introduce music that uses these techniques.

STANDARD 2A

Performing on instruments, alone and with others, a varied repertoire of music:
Students perform with expression and technical accuracy a large and varied repertoire
of instrumental literature with a level of difficulty of 4, on a scale of 1 to 6.

Objective

- Students will play with expression and technical accuracy ensemble music with a level of difficulty of 4, for barred (mallet) percussion instruments, recorders, and untuned hand percussion instruments.

Materials

- *Colores: Six Pièces pour Instruments à Percussion et Flûtes à bec* by Jos Wuytack (Editions Musicales Alphonse Leduc, 175, rue Saint-Honoré, Paris), Level 4 (first two pieces)

- Barred Orff instruments (soprano and alto glockenspiels; soprano, alto, and bass xylophones; soprano, alto, and bass metallophones—three mallets per metallophone)

- Tambourine

- Claves or woodblock

- Soprano recorders

- Alto recorders

Prior Knowledge and Experiences

- Students have played mallet percussion instruments and recorders and a varied repertoire of music with a level of difficulty of 4.

Procedures

1. Give all students the score for *Colores.* Have them identify the meters (2/4, 3/4, and 6/8) and the rhythmic and melodic patterns in the music. Then have them speak the rhythmic patterns using a syllable such as "doo."

2. Ask individual students to demonstrate the rhythmic and melodic patterns on the appropriate instruments.

3. Organize students into two ensembles. Have Ensemble 1 work on the section titled "Contrasts," with three players working on the A part while four others work on the B part; the bass xylophone player works initially with the A group but then rotates between the A and B groups. Subdivide Ensemble 2 into a mallet percussion group and a recorder group to work on the section titled "Bells of Joy." Have at least two students play glockenspiels and three play metallophones (up to eight glockenspiels may be used). Have all students not playing a mallet instrument in Ensemble 2 play soprano or alto recorder. Assign one student the role of chairperson in each ensemble's groups. Rotate among the groups to assist the students.

4. Have each group from both ensembles perform its part for the class. Encourage students to listen to each other as they play and to respond to the interplay of the parts. After each group has played, have the other students listen, discuss, and evaluate the playing for expression and technical accuracy.

5. Have the groups join together in their ensembles and practice their parts, keeping in mind the suggestions the class has made. Assist students as necessary, reminding them of the class's suggestions.

6. Have each ensemble perform its section for the other ensemble. Elicit suggestions from the listening ensemble. Then have students form ensembles with one student per part to perform the music.

Indicators of Success

- Students demonstrate the understanding and skills necessary for successful ensemble performance by playing "Colores" on percussion instruments with technical accuracy and expression.

(continued)

Follow-up

- Have students consider the contrasting tone color of the two sections they played and compare them with the tone colors of other sections in *Colores*. Discuss with them the use of form and musical characteristics such as unity and variety, ostinatos, and dynamic contrasts.

- When students are able to perform the pieces well, have them record the pieces and respond to them through the visual arts, the literary arts, or dance with the help of the respective teachers.

STANDARD 2B

Performing on instruments, alone and with others, a varied repertoire of music: Students perform an appropriate part in an ensemble, demonstrating well-developed ensemble skills.

Objective

- Students will read and play music for hand drums and recorders, showing both individual musical independence and ability to perform as an ensemble with technical accuracy and expression.

Materials

- *For Hand Drums and Recorders* by Isabel McNeill Carley (Allison Park, PA: Music Innovations, 1982)
- Hand drums
- Sopranino, soprano, alto, and tenor recorders

Prior Knowledge and Experiences

- Students have played hand drums and recorders in general music classes.

Procedures

1. Ask students to read about and experiment individually with the ambidextrous hand drum technique on page 37 in *For Hand Drums and Recorders.*

2. Have students perform together on hand drums the exercises on page 37 and then identify any musical or technical problems. Ask them to repeat the exercises, correcting the problems identified.

3. Have students select recorders (sopranino, soprano, alto, or tenor) and sightread the melody to "Pavane," by Jean Tabouret, on page 38, reviewing fingerings as needed. Have students playing F instruments (sopranino and alto) transpose an octave up.

4. Divide the class into two groups and have them play page 38 as written with hand drums and recorders. Then have groups switch parts so that all students have ensemble experience with both parts.

5. Discuss with students the historical background and performance practice indicated by the title "Pavane" and the date (1589).

6. Discuss with students the expressive markings in the piece, emphasizing the importance of a uniform interpretation of the expressive markings. Also, discuss the importance of listening to other parts and players in ensemble playing. Then ask them to play the piece again with more focus on style and expression and on listening to others.

7. Ask students to evaluate their own performance and that of the whole class and make suggestions for improvement. Have students keep the suggestions in mind and play the piece once more, focusing on style and expression.

Indicators of Success

- Students perform the music with technical accuracy and expression on hand drums and recorders.
- Students demonstrate improvement in their ensemble skills as they listen more to each other and focus on playing accurately and expressively.

(continued)

Follow-up

- Have students analyze "Hungarian Dance," by Jacob de la Paix, 1607 (pages 39–40 of *For Hand Drums and Recorders*). Ask them to identify the similarities and differences between this piece and "Pavane." Then have them learn to play the piece on recorders and hand drums.

- Form small ensembles with one student on a part for both pieces that students have learned.

STANDARD 2B

Performing on instruments, alone and with others, a varied repertoire of music: Students perform an appropriate part in an ensemble, demonstrating well-developed ensemble skills.

Objective

■ Students will perform in a percussion ensemble, making proper entrances, performing rhythms with precision, keeping a steady beat, and listening to other parts for appropriate balance.

Materials

■ "Junkanoo Rhythms," in *The Music Connection,* Grade 8 (Parsippany, NJ: Silver Burdett Ginn, 1995)

■ Four cowbells

■ Medium skin drum

■ Low skin drum

■ Two whistles

■ Car rim

■ Party horn

Prior Knowledge and Experiences

■ Students can perform basic rhythms in 4/4 meter.

■ Students have played a variety of percussion instruments.

Procedures

1. Have students echo clap rhythm patterns in "Junkanoo Rhythms."

2. Have students practice each part by looking at and thinking about the notation, chanting the rhythms, and tapping their hands on their desks as if playing the instrument. As they do each step successfully, select students to play an instrument for each pattern and to continue playing the pattern as other instruments are added, proceeding from simpler to more difficult rhythms (that is, low skin drum, cowbell 1, cowbell 2, whistle 1, medium skin drum, cowbells hit together, whistle 2, car rim, party horn).

3. When students demonstrate confidence in playing the rhythms, point out the staggered entrances of the instruments and explain the importance of keeping a steady beat in the ensemble and executing each rhythm with precision. Then have students play "Junkanoo Rhythms" as notated.

4. After measure 46, have everyone improvise new rhythms on their instruments.

5. Discuss with students other percussion "instruments" they could bring from home to add to the ensemble.

6. Tell students about the Junkanoo cultural festival of the Bahamas, a street festival similar to Mardi Gras. Explain the ululating, high-pitched vocal trills that people in the Bahamas frequently add to enhance the festivities as they join the processions down the street.

7. Encourage students to listen carefully to the interplay of rhythms in "Junkanoo Rhythms" and to feel their own rhythm contributing one thread to the overall texture. Explain the importance of listening to each other, both to ensure that they play together and to ensure that all parts can be heard. Then have them perform the piece again while moving in shuffling or strutting steps to imitate the processions in the Bahamas. Remind them to add their voices in some ululating trills as the ensemble sounds reach an exciting level.

(continued)

Indicators of Success

- Students play "Junkanoo Rhythms" on percussion instruments, entering with their instruments at the appropriate time, executing rhythm patterns with precision, and listening to each other to improve their ensemble playing.

Follow-up

- Have students research the Junkanoo cultural festival of the Bahamas.

- Have students exchange instruments for "Junkanoo Rhythms." Ask them to teach the rhythm they know to the instrument's new player.

- Have students learn to sing and play other songs and rhythms from the Caribbean that use similar patterns.

Performing on instruments, alone and with others, a varied repertoire of music: Students perform an appropriate part in an ensemble, demonstrating well-developed ensemble skills.

Objective

- Students will play a piece in a steel drum band with technical accuracy and good ensemble skills.

Materials

- Steel drums (soprano, alto, baritone, bass)

- Transparencies or individual music sheets containing a four-part arrangement of "Feliz Navidad," by Jose Feliciano, preferably written by the teacher so that it is appropriate for the students; song source: *Share the Music*, Grade 5 (New York: Macmillan/McGraw-Hill, 1995) or *The Music Connection*, Grade 7 (Parsippany, NJ: Silver Burdett Ginn, 1995); see accompanying example for arrangement ideas

- Overhead projector, if transparencies are used

Prior Knowledge and Experiences

- Students have had some experience playing the steel drums and can relate the notes on the staff to their drums.

- Students have studied music theory.

Procedures

1. Display the transparency or distribute the music sheets with the arrangement of "Feliz Navidad." Have students sightsing the melody, or teach the melody by rote.

2. Check to see that each student knows how to play each note on the staff on the drum. Then have the students review the rhythms in the music by speaking and clapping them.

3. Have students work on their parts individually. Then ask all those playing the same part to play together, having one group play at a time. Have each group identify any problems and make corrections.

4. Have two parts, then three parts, and then the entire ensemble play the piece. Help students to identify and improve the phrases or sections that need extra work.

5. Ask the entire ensemble to play the piece again, listening to the other parts and responding to the interplay of the parts.

6. Ask students how the playing could be more expressive (for example, with a different tempo or dynamics). Have them experiment with their suggestions.

7. Have students decide which suggestions to incorporate into their playing. Then have the entire ensemble play the piece while listening to the other parts, responding to the interplay of the parts, and playing accurately and expressively.

Indicators of Success

- Students start and finish together.

- Students play their parts with accurate pitches and rhythms and appropriate expression.

- Students respond as an ensemble to the interplay of the parts.

(continued)

Follow-up

- Have students listen to recordings of steel bands and learn to play other pieces that are suitable for steel band arrangements and that require increased musical skills. When they have learned several pieces, have them perform them for parents, teachers, or other students.

Feliz Navidad

José Feliciano
Arr. Lloyd P. Hoover

STANDARD 2C

Performing on instruments, alone and with others, a varied repertoire of music:
Students perform in small ensembles with one student on a part.

Objective

- Students will perform a duet in pairs on guitars.

Materials

- "Chiapanecas," in *Alfred's Basic Guitar Method*, Book 1 (Van Nuys, CA: Alfred Publishing Company, 1959)
- Guitars

Prior Knowledge and Experiences

- Students can play in the first position on guitar.
- Students have studied music theory.

Procedures

1. Review with students 3/4 meter and the number of beats the following receive in that meter: quarter note, quarter rest, dotted-half note. Then have students count and clap the rhythms in parts 1 and 2 of "Chiapanecas."

2. Ask students to compare parts 1 and 2, noting specifically where the parts have different rhythms. Then have them analyze the chords for each part and play them on their guitars.

3. Have students say the letter names aloud, in rhythm, for both parts. Have them do this again as they finger the notes on their guitars.

4. Ask students to explain the dynamic markings at the beginning of the piece and to describe how the dynamics should change as they play the piece.

5. Have all students practice part 1 of the duet. Then have all students practice part 2.

6. Have pairs of students take turns performing the duet for the class. While each pair plays, have the other students listen to evaluate the players' expressiveness and technical accuracy. Then ask listeners to give feedback to the players. Have each pair play again, implementing their peers' suggestions.

Indicators of Success

- Students perform "Chiapanecas" in pairs as a duet with technical accuracy and expressiveness.

Follow-up

- Have students continue to develop their music reading skills and guitar skills as they learn second position on the guitar.
- Have students listen to recordings of Mexican mariachi bands as well as classical guitarists and compare their technique and the expressiveness of their playing with that of the performers on the recordings.

STANDARD 2C

Performing on instruments, alone and with others, a varied repertoire of music:
Students perform in small ensembles with one student on a part.

Objective

- Students will play a trio on recorders with one person on a part and with technical accuracy and expression.

Materials

- "Helas Madame" by King Henry VIII of England, in *Renaissance Time Pieces and Dances,* arr. Gerald Burakoff and Willy Strickland (Fort Worth, TX: Sweet Pipes, 1983)

- Soprano and alto recorders

Prior Knowledge and Experiences

- Students have played beginning-level music on soprano and alto recorders.

Procedures

1. Divide the three parts of "Helas Madame" among the students. Then have them examine the notation for their specific part and identify which phrases are the same or similar.

2. Review the fingerings on the recorder with the students. Have them finger the notes for their respective parts rhythmically in a slow tempo.

3. Have students play their parts together once. Isolate the parts that need extra attention and have students practice those parts. Then have them play the piece again.

4. Ask students to speculate on why King Henry VIII wrote this piece, and ask them with what sort of expression they think it should be played. Have them play the piece together, with two pulses per measure, to achieve the sprightly style characteristic of much Renaissance music. Discuss how the emotion of the piece can be expressed in their playing (for example, by varying dynamics and tempo).

5. Divide students into groups of three to practice together as trios. Then have each trio play for the class as the class evaluates the accuracy and expressiveness of the playing.

Indicators of Success

- Students play "Helas Madame" in recorder trios with technical accuracy and expression.

Follow-up

- Give students the opportunity to play tenor and bass recorders. Have them form chamber groups and listen to and report on both vocal and instrumental Renaissance music. (For example: "Did people in Renaissance times value music differently than people do today?") If possible, have students share their projects with students in English classes studying Shakespeare or in history classes studying the Renaissance.

STANDARD 2C

STRATEGY 3 OF 3

Performing on instruments, alone and with others, a varied repertoire of music:
Students perform in small ensembles with one student on a part.

Objective

- Students will play a piece in a steel drum band with one student on a part and with expression and technical accuracy.

Materials

- Steel drums (soprano, alto, baritone, bass)

- Transparencies or individual music sheets containing a four-part arrangement of "Water Come a Me Eye" (preferably written by the teacher so that arrangement is appropriate for students); song source: *World of Music*, Grade 7 (Parsippany, NJ: Silver Burdett Ginn, 1991); see accompanying example for arrangement ideas

- Overhead projector, if transparencies are used

Prior Knowledge and Experiences

- Students have studied music theory.

- Students can distinguish between the soprano, alto, baritone, and bass steel drums.

- Students have had some experience playing the steel drums and can relate the notes on the staff to their drums.

Procedures

1. Show the transparency (or distribute the music sheet) with the arrangement of "Water Come a Me Eye" for soprano, alto, baritone, and bass drums. Have students sightsing the melody, or teach them the melody by rote.

2. Assign each student to one of the drums. Help students find the pitches on their drums for their parts in the song.

3. Have students work on their parts individually. Then ask all those playing the soprano drum to play together, then alto, then baritone, and then bass. After each group has played its part, have students assess the accuracy of their playing, identify problems, and make corrections.

4. Have two parts, then three parts, and then the entire ensemble play the piece.

5. Ask students how the playing could be more expressive. Discuss whether a different tempo or dynamics would enhance the performance. Have students experiment with the suggestions.

6. Finally, ask quartets of students to play the piece, listening to the other parts, responding to the interplay of the parts, and working toward an accurate and expressive performance. Ask listeners to give feedback to the players. Then have quartets play again, implementing their peers' suggestions.

Indicators of Success

- Students play accurate pitches and rhythms in their steel drum performance of "Water Come a Me Eye" with one student on a part.

- Students start and finish together.

- Students determine an appropriate tempo and dynamics and play the piece expressively.

(continued)

Follow-up

- Have students listen to recordings of Caribbean steel bands, and focus their listening on the ensemble playing of the performers.
- Have students learn to play other steel band arrangements that require increased musical skills.

Water Come a Me Eye

Jamaican Folk Song
Arr. Lloyd P. Hoover

STANDARD 3A

Improvising melodies, variations, and accompaniments: Students *improvise stylistically appropriate harmonizing parts.*

Objective

- Students will sing and harmonize an African American spiritual, improvising with tones from the tonic and dominant chords.

Materials

- "Over My Head," in *Share the Music,* Grade 5 (New York: Macmillan/McGraw-Hill, 1995); or *Get America Singing . . . Again!* (Milwaukee: Hal Leonard Corporation, 1996)
- Chalkboard

Prior Knowledge and Experiences

- Students can sing the African American spiritual "Over My Head" in unison.
- Students have studied tonic and dominant seventh chords, understand the terms "root," "third," "fifth," and "seventh," and can sing each of the chord tones.
- Students have been introduced to "passing tones" and "neighbor tones."

Procedures

1. Have students review "Over My Head" by singing it in unison as you accompany on the keyboard using tonic and dominant chords. Then write the tonic and dominant seventh chords in the key of F major on the chalkboard, having students tell you what notes to use. Divide the class into voice parts (soprano, alto, tenor, and bass) and have students sing the chords, first in unison as broken chords and then as block chords in harmony.

2. Play a I–V7 chord progression on the keyboard (for example, I - V7 - I - I - I - V7 - V7 - I), and have students identify chord changes by responding to tonic chords with hands on knees and dominant chords with hands in the air. Then ask students to respond in the same way as you play the melody of "Over My Head" with a I–V7 accompaniment.

3. Have students sing the roots of the I and V7 chords—"one," "five," "one," " five," etc.—as you signal with one or five fingers. Then have them sing the roots of the chords as you softly sing the song and signal the chord changes with one or five fingers.

4. Ask the men to sing the chord roots as the rest of the class sings the melody. Then have the men substitute repeated words ("joy" or "somewhere") or the words of the song for "one" and "five." Select some treble voices to harmonize in thirds above the melody. Add a third harmony part by asking some treble voices to sing the fifth of the tonic chord (*sol*) and the seventh of the dominant chord (*fa*), using a repeated word or the words of the song.

5. Have students practice the song with the three parts harmonizing the melody. Then have students switch parts so that everyone gets a chance to improvise a harmony.

6. Have students keep singing the song and experiment by including other chord tones, passing tones, and neighbor tones for harmony parts. Have them also improvise responses during held notes and rests (for example, "Yes! Over my head!"). Assure them that it is all right to make mistakes as they experiment.

7. Have small groups improvise harmonies while one student sings the melody. Then ask these groups to sing for the class. Invite student comments on which improvisations seem effective and why.

(continued)

Indicators of Success

■ Students improvise harmony parts with full voices using tones from tonic and dominant chords as they sing "Over My Head."

Follow-up

■ Have students harmonize other African American spirituals, such as "Rock-a-My Soul," "He's Got the Whole World in His Hands," and "Mary and Martha," as well as songs from the Caribbean, such as "Mary Ann" and "Yellow Bird."

■ Have students listen to recordings of spirituals sung by African Americans, such as those in Bernice Johnson Reagon, *Wade in the Water: African American Sacred Music Traditions,* with teacher's guide (Washington, DC: National Public Radio, 1994), and *Spirituals in Concert,* Kathleen Battle and Jessye Norman (Deutsche Grammophon 429790-2). Then have them harmonize songs that also include subdominant harmony, such as "Oh, Freedom," in *The Music Connection* (Parsippany, NJ: Siver Burdett Ginn, 1995), Grade 8.

STANDARD 3B

Improvising melodies, variations, and accompaniments: Students improvise rhythmic and melodic variations on given pentatonic melodies and melodies in major and minor keys.

Objective

- Students will improvise melodies on a given melody using the black keys on the keyboard.

Materials

- Keyboard for each student
- Large keyboard chart for the front of the room
- Grand Staff chart
- Small keyboard charts for each student
- Small Grand Staff charts for each student

Prior Knowledge and Experiences

- Students have studied music theory.
- Students can name the black and white keys on the keyboard.

Procedures

1. Demonstrate for students the proper keyboard playing position. Have them take their places at their keyboards, give them a steady pulse, and ask them to play clusters of two black keys and three black keys, going hand over hand with any fingers the range of the keyboard, always keeping a steady beat. Ask them to repeat the exercise while naming the white keys (referring to keyboard charts) around the clusters of black keys (that is, CDE—FGAB—CDE—FGAB, etc.).

2. Direct students' attention to the large Grand Staff chart and have them examine the Grand Staff and the letter names of the notes and how these relate to the keyboard. Call out specific notes in a random order for the students to play. Then call out two or more notes at once. Finally, call out motives from familiar songs, such as: "D-G-G-G" ("Here Comes the Bride"), or "C-C-D-C-F-E" ("Happy Birthday"), or the beginning of the school song.

3. Have students speak the rhythm of "Happy Birthday" on a syllable such as "doo." Then ask them to play that rhythm on the black keys, improvising a new melody.

4. Help students to realize that their improvisations will have more coherence if they repeat and vary melodic patterns. Ask them to improvise again on the black keys to the rhythm of "Happy Birthday," but to repeat and vary their melodic patterns.

5. Ask students to practice their improvised melodies several times so that they can remember them.

6. Have individual students play their melodies for the class as other students listen and provide feedback. Then have students apply the suggestions from their peers and play their pieces again.

Indicators of Success

- Students improvise melodies with repeated patterns on the black keys of the keyboard.

(continued)

Follow-up

■ Have students play five-finger melodies, such as those in *Group Piano for Adults,* Book 1, by E. L. Lancaster and Kenon D. Renfrow (Van Nuys, CA; Alfred Publishing Company, 1995), or *PianoLab: An Introduction to Class Piano,* 3rd ed., by Carolynn A. Lindeman (Belmont, CA; Wadsworth Publishing Company, 1996). Then have them improvise similar melodies.

Improvising melodies, variations, and accompaniments: Students improvise original melodies over given chord progressions, each in a consistent style, meter, and tonality.

Objective

- Students will improvise a melody over the tonic-dominant accompaniment to a simple folk song.

Materials

- Keyboards or keyboard-type instruments
- Chalkboard
- Manuscript paper

Prior Knowledge and Experiences

- Students have studied triad construction and the tonic-dominant harmony relationship.
- Students have been introduced to "passing tones" and "neighbor tones."

Procedures

1. Write the melody of the French folk song "The Bridge of Avignon" on the chalkboard in the key of F major (see melody in figure 1), and have students notate it on manuscript paper. Have students learn the melody of this French folk song by singing or by playing instruments while reading the notation on the board. If the students sing, have them use solfège, letter names, or scale degree numbers.

2. Have students examine the melody to discover that it is in F major, that it uses a range of pitches that extends from *sol* below the tonic to *sol* above the tonic, and that it is composed of only eighth-note and quarter-note rhythms. Then have students notate the pitches of the tonic (F) triad in the treble clef. Ask them to try to play or sing the melody as you play an accompaniment with only the tonic chord, helping them to discover that a harmony change must occur to accommodate the melody.

3. Ask students to circle in their notated melodies the first pitch occurring on the strong beat of each measure. Explain that a harmony change must occur at these places to accommodate the melodic line.

4. Have students notate the dominant chord (C) in this piece. Tell them that in traditional Western music, a harmony change to the dominant is signaled by the second or seventh tone of a scale (*re* or *ti*) on an accented beat.

5. Have students notate the tonic-dominant harmonic pattern indicated by the melody by writing in chord roots only (F or C) below the melody. Each measure will have one chord root, except the final measure, which has two. (See figure 1.)

6. On keyboards, ask students to improvise a simple melody using pitches of the tonic and dominant triads other than those used in "The Bridge of Avignon" on the strong beats of each measure. Have them use the tonic-dominant pattern from "The Bridge of Avignon" for the accompaniment. Suggest that they use half notes and quarter notes, paralleling the rhythm of the accompaniment, for their melodies. (For example, see figure 2.)

(continued)

7. Encourage students to embellish and elaborate their simple melodies. Tell them that they may begin to move among the tones of the tonic or dominant triads in quarter or eighth notes or that they may begin to add upper and lower neighbor and passing tones. Remind them that the first sound in each measure must be a member of the tonic or dominant triad. Have them perform their improvisations for each other, eliciting discussion and evaluation.

Indicators of Success

- Students derive a bass line from the harmonic implications of a given tonic-dominant melody.

- Students improvise melodies over the given bass line.

Follow-up

- As students develop more facility in improvisation, have them incorporate elements of tempo, melodic direction, and melodic flow to make their melodies more interesting.

Figure 1. "The Bridge of Avignon."

Figure 2. *Example of improvised melody over tonic-dominant accompaniment.*

STANDARD 3C

Improvising melodies, variations, and accompaniments: Students improvise original melodies over given chord progressions, each in a consistent style, meter, and tonality.

Objective

- Students will use an electronic keyboard to improvise melodic variations on a simple melody in a consistent style, meter, and tonality.

Materials

- Electronic keyboards for each student, preferably with headphones
- Copies of "Jammin'" (see accompanying music example)
- Chalkboard

Prior Knowledge and Experiences

- Students can play simple melodies on the electronic keyboard and are familiar with the switches, the tone bank, and the beat bank.
- Students can write tonic, dominant, and subdominant chords.
- Students have been introduced to "neighbor tones."
- Students have learned "Jammin'" on the keyboard and have selected an instrument (for example, electric piano or electric bass) from the tone bank to play the melody and a beat (for example, rock or funk) from the beat bank for the rhythm.

Procedures

1. Tell students that they are going to improvise on the melody of "Jammin'," using the instruments and beats they selected in a previous class. Explain that they should not change the pitch on the first beat of a measure. Suggest that they change the rhythm by using eighth notes or dotted rhythms, for example. Suggest also that they use some neighbor tones.

   Walk around and listen to what the students do, helping them to stick to the style of the original piece.

2. Explain to students that the first phrase of "Jammin'" is built on the C chord: C-E-G. Have them play that chord with the right hand. Then have them improvise the first phrase again, this time using E or G on the first beat of the measure.

3. Ask students on what chord the second phrase begins. Have them play an F chord—F-A-C—with the right hand. Then have them improvise two measures on the F chord, this time having them use A or C on the first beat of the measure. Have them finish the phrase by improvising on the C chord.

4. Ask students on what chord the third phrase begins. Have them play a G chord—G-B-D. Then have them improvise two measures using tones of that chord. Have them finish the piece by improvising on the C chord.

5. Explain to students that music frequently uses repeated patterns. Have them decide on one rhythmic pattern they could use in their individual improvisations on the "Jammin'" melody. Show them at least one rhythmic example on the board, such as the following:

   (continued)

6. Have students experiment with their improvisations until they discover something they like and can play smoothly.

7. Ask students to improvise for the class, and have the class offer suggestions and comments.

Indicators of Success

- Students create improvisations on "Jammin'" on an electronic keyboard with attention to style, meter, and tonality.

Follow-up

- Have students use their electronic keyboards to improvise on simple melodies that they create.

- Have students listen to and discuss recordings of jazz artists improvising on melodies familiar to them (for example: Variations on "Yankee Doodle" by Joseph Joubert, *The Music Connection,* Grade 5 (Parsippany, NJ: Silver Burdett Ginn, 1995); "I Got Rhythm" by George and Ira Gershwin, performed by Don Byas (tenor saxophone), from *The Smithsonian Collection of Classic Jazz,* revised edition, selected and annotated by Martin Williams, Atlantic SD-310; "Don't Worry, Be Happy" by Bobby McFerrin, from *1988 Billboard Top Hits,* Rhino Records R2-7164.

Jammin'

STANDARD 3C

Improvising melodies, variations, and accompaniments: *Students improvise original melodies over given chord progressions, each in a consistent style, meter, and tonality.*

Objective

- Students will perform a vocal improvisation on a 12-bar blues progression.

Materials

- Chalkboard
- Hand-held microphone

Prior Knowledge and Experiences

- Students have studied music theory.
- Students have studied vocal technique.

Procedures

1. Write the following motive on the chalkboard:

   Have students echo as you sing the motive, pointing to each note of the motive as everyone sings it.

2. Have students sing the motive, listening carefully to see whether the flatted tones and half steps are in tune. Model the notes that were not in tune and have students echo. Continue until students perform the motive accurately.

3. Play a I-IV-V blues progression in the key of C on the keyboard and sing the motive with it, transposing the motive for the F and G chords. Then have the students join you. Finally, have them sing the motive alone with the blues progression.

4. Have each student sing the motive alone while you play the blues progression. Encourage applause for each individual's effort.

5. Have students sing the motive one more time while you improvise a short vocal motive (a "scat") for the first measure of the break (see measures 3 and 4 of the music example), using only the notes in the scale they have been singing. Have students echo your scat singing on the second measure of the break. Do this call-and-response exercise four to six times.

6. Have individual students try their own scat singing on the two-measure break. Let them know that they can use only a few notes at first, just those in the descending blues scale they have been singing. Tell everyone that they must sing something—even if it is only one note repeated in a varied rhythm—and have each student do at least two improvisations. Encourage applause for each student's singing.

(continued)

7. Invite individual students to scat freely against the progression using the microphone. Explain that they may sing the motive again with just one or two altered notes or they may improvise freely not using the motive at all—or anything in between to create a new melody. Have everyone perform at least one scat. Again, encourage applause for each effort.

Indicators of Success

- Students improvise a short scat using the tones of the blues scale.

Follow-up

- Have students listen to recordings of other jazz artists, such as Billie Holiday, Ella Fitzgerald, and Sarah Vaughan, and try to imitate their styles as they continue scat singing on repeated chord progressions in a variety of keys.

STANDARD 3D

Advanced

Improvising melodies, variations, and accompaniments: Students improvise stylistically appropriate harmonizing parts in a variety of styles.

Objective

- Students will sing an African American spiritual, improvising harmonizing parts with tones from the tonic, subdominant, and dominant-seventh chords.

Materials

- Notation for melody of "Down by the Riverside," with lead sheet notation; song source: *The Music Connection*, Grades 5 and 8 (Parsippany, NJ: Silver Burdett Ginn, 1995), or *Share the Music*, Grade 4 (New York: Macmillan/McGraw-Hill, 1995)

- Chalkboard

Prior Knowledge and Experiences

- Students have sung "Down by the Riverside" in unison.

- Students have studied tonic, subdominant, and dominant-seventh chords and understand the terms "root," "third," "fifth," and "seventh."

- Students have been introduced to "passing tones" and "neighbor tones."

- Students have studied solfège and the Kodály hand signs.

Procedures

1. Have students sing "Down by the Riverside" in unison as a review as you accompany on the keyboard with tonic, subdominant, and dominant chords. Then have volunteers identify and write the pitches in those three chords on the board. Ask students to sing the chords, first one tone at a time and then as chords.

2. Have students identify chord changes in "Down by the Riverside" as you play it slowly with a I-IV-V7 chordal accompaniment. Have them put their hands on their knees when they hear the tonic chord, put their hands up in the air when they hear the dominant-seventh chord, and put their hands out in front of them when they hear the subdominant chord.

3. Ask students to sing the roots of the chords as they do the hand signs and as you point to the chord roots on the board. Have students continue singing and signing the chord roots as you softly sing the song and signal the chord changes by pointing to the chords on the board. Point out that the melody emphasizes chord tones of the same chords for which they are singing the roots.

4. Ask basses to sing the chord roots using the syllables *do, fa,* and *sol,* while the rest of the class sings the melody softly. Then have basses substitute the word "down" for the syllables while the class sings the melody. Have a student go to the board and shade in the chord roots that the basses are singing. Note to students that the other tones in the chords are available for harmonizing.

5. Help students find an easy treble harmony to sing by using *mi* when they hear the tonic chord and changing to only one other pitch (*fa*) when they hear the dominant-seventh and subdominant chords. Reinforce this by having a student shade in the third of the tonic chord (*mi* on the board) and the seventh of the dominant seventh chord (*fa* on the board). Point out that *fa* is the root of the subdominant chord. Have the treble voices sing and sign *mi* and *fa,* changing from one note to the other as the harmony changes, while the others sing the melody softly. Repeat, this time having the treble voices substitute the word "down" for the syllables.

(continued)

6. Add a third harmony part by asking other voices to sing the fifth of the tonic chord (*sol*), staying on the same pitch for the dominant chord and then moving to *la* or *do* on the subdominant chord.

7. Have the students sing the song in four parts: three parts harmonizing and one part singing the melody. Ask them to harmonize again, this time feeling free to move to other chord tones or to add neighbor tones and passing tones. Emphasize that it is all right to make mistakes as they try their harmonizing skills. Encourage improvised responses where the melody has held notes or rests. Have soloists sing the melody as others harmonize and improvise in parts.

Indicators of Success

■ Students improvise harmony parts for "Down by the Riverside," using pitches from the tonic, subdominant, and dominant chords.

Follow-up

■ Have students improvise harmonies for other songs having I-IV-V7 harmony, such as "This Land Is Your Land," "Michael Row the Boat Ashore," "Yellow Bird," "Gonna Get Along Without You Now," "Oh, Freedom," and "Blowin' in the Wind."

Improvising melodies, variations, and accompaniments: Students improvise original melodies in a variety of styles, over given chord progressions, each in a consistent style, meter, and tonality.

Objective

■ Students will improvise, vocally or instrumentally, original melodies over a two-chord progression in the key of C major.

Materials

■ Keyboard (keyboards for students are optional)

■ Computer and MIDI-compatible synthesizer or tone module (if available)

■ Computer accompaniment program, such as Band in a Box (Buffalo, NY: PG Music) (if available)

■ Prerecorded accompaniment tracks, such as *Major and Minor,* vol. 24 of Jamey Aebersold's *A New Approach to Jazz Improvisation,* Jamey Aebersold Jazz, PO Box 1244C, New Albany, IN 47151 (if computer or accompaniment program is not available)

■ Chalkboard with Cmaj7 chord and Dm7/G chord (Dm7 over a G in the bass)

Procedures

1. Play individual chords (for example, Cmaj7 or Dm7/G) on the keyboard without a steady beat and ask students to try to hear three- or four-note patterns that fit each chord. Suggest that students imagine different melodies, such as four notes going up, or two notes up and two notes down, or moving by steps only, or using at least one skip.

2. Have volunteers sing the melodies they hear. Be positive and non-judgmental; whatever they sing at this point is acceptable.

3. Have students listen to the preprogrammed two-chord accompaniment "groove" of the computer accompaniment program with alternating measures of Cmaj7, Dm7/G. Use pop or Latin style with straight eighth notes for the first experience.

4. As students listen again to the two-chord accompaniment, point to the chord tones on the chalkboard and have them sing (or play scale patterns on the white keys) in whole, half, quarter, and eighth notes. Students may sing using solfège or with scat sounds ("duh-buh-duh"). They will quickly discover that almost any note at any given time either fits with the accompaniment or is right next to one that does.

5. Still using the accompaniment, have students respond in a "call-and-response" manner by improvising two-measure melodies that complement melodies you play or sing. Allow several students or the whole class to improvise simultaneously. Then, when they are more comfortable, have them improvise individually.

6. After students have improvised alone, with the accompaniment, have them alternately improvise first two-measure phrases and then four-measure phrases in a call-and-response style with you doing the call. The accompaniment program will allow you to readily change styles or tempi to keep the accompaniment musically fresh and interesting for the students.

(continued)

Prior Knowledge and Experiences

- Students have listened to examples of jazz performances featuring modal improvisation (for example, Miles Davis's "Kind of Blue" or Herbie Hancock's "Maiden Voyage").

- Students have analyzed the music and improvisations to which they have listened.

- Students have had experience playing classroom keyboard or mallet instruments.

Indicators of Success

- Students improvise two- or four-measure melodies vocally or instrumentally over a two-chord progression in the key of C major to a variety of accompaniments.

Follow-up

- Have students create a sixteen-measure improvisation over the two-chord progression in the style and tempo of their choice.

Improvising melodies, variations, and accompaniments: Students improvise original melodies in a variety of styles, over given chord progressions, each in a consistent style, meter, and tonality.

Objective

- Students will improvise a chaconne on instruments, using the decorated-third approach to melodic development.

Materials

- Classroom melody instruments such as Orff instruments (xylophone, metallophone), recorders, keyboards, or traditional wind and string instruments
- Chalkboard

Prior Knowledge and Experiences

- Students can identify by sight and sound major, minor, and diminished triads.
- Students have developed basic improvisation skills.
- Students have studied what a chaconne is.

Procedures

1. Give each student an instrument. Have students play the root pitches of the following ascending triads:

Then have them play the pitches of each triad as broken chords identifying the quality of each (major, minor, diminished).

2. Have students examine the following example:

Tell them that the diminished triad, based on the sixth degree of this mode—Dorian—is eliminated from the pattern of perfect fifths because of its harmonic instability (that is, its tendency to need resolution). Explain also that the closing triad movement is embellished to create a cadence. Ask students to observe the 3/4 meter signature and then to play the root and fifth of each triad together, leaving out the third, as in the example.

3. Divide the class into two sections. Have some students perform the pattern of moving fifths while others play the thirds an octave higher, creating new voicings of the triads and cadencing at the proper time.

(or 8va higher)

(continued)

4. Discuss with students ways to ornament the line created by the extracted thirds. Use this example to stimulate ideas:

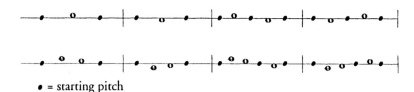

• = starting pitch

Explain to students that they can use neighboring tones, stepwise movement, skips to other triad tones, and so on, as they see in the example, and that the goal is to create a lyrical melody in 3/4 time from this set of pitch contours. Tell them that this method of creating a melody is known as "decoration of the third," and it is found in the keyboard and lute music of seventeenth-century Elizabethan composers. The triads are nonfunctional and are often used in a parallel movement.

5. Have students improvise for each other, and elicit discussion and evaluation. Then have some students perform the moving fifth patterns in the bass while others take turns at improvising melodies based on the extracted thirds an octave or more above the bass. Remind students that the third of the triad must sound along with the open fifth on the strong beat of each measure until the melody cadences.

Indicators of Success

- Students improvise chaconnes using the decorated-third approach.
- Students demonstrate their understanding of the decorated-third approach in their evaluations of the improvisations.

Follow-up

- Suggest that students continue to develop their improvisations by adding rhythmic motives to the moving fifths, by separating the fifths between two instruments, by adding nonpitched percussion instruments, or by adding open fifths above the improvisation at various triads in the sequence.
- Have students form small ensembles and perform their improvitions for the class.

STANDARD 4A

Composing and arranging music within specified guidelines: Students compose music in several distinct styles, demonstrating creativity in using the elements of music for expressive effect.

Objective

■ Students will collaborate to create a composition for percussion ensemble, synthesizer, and computer.

Materials

■ Percussion instruments

■ Computer (IBM-compatible with Windows, or Macintosh)

■ Synthesizer

■ Sequencing program such as *Vision* (Palo Alto, CA: Opcode Systems)

■ Publishing program such as *Finale*™ (Eden Praire, MN: Coda Music Technology)

■ Blank audiocassette tapes

■ Audio-recording and -playback equipment

Prior Knowledge and Experiences

■ Students have played acoustic percussion instruments.

■ Students can notate many of the rhythms they have played.

Procedures

1. Work with students using the computer and a synthesizer to create a series of musical sequences with melodies, harmonies, and bass lines in a variety of meters.

2. Record on audiocassette tapes the completed series "a tempo" and at a slower tempo. Then distribute these tapes to students.

3. Have each student create sixteen rhythmic units for a particular percussion instrument, making each unit one measure long and in the same meters and tempi as the recorded sequences.

4. Ask students to hand in their papers with the rhythmic units they have created and notated. Assemble the examples on the computer into repetitive groupings to form motives, sequences, phrases, and periods. The assembled product should match the form, meters, and tempi of the recorded sequences.

5. Print out the various parts and distribute them to students. Have them identify their own units and discuss how those units have been arranged into the larger piece and why they are where they are.

6. Rehearse the assembled piece with students.

7. Have students perform the final product on percussion instruments with the computer and synthesizer.

Indicators of Success

■ Students collaborate to create short rhythmic units for percussion instruments.

■ Students describe how their rhythmic units fit into the larger work.

■ Students perform their parts on percussion instruments in the assembled piece.

Follow-up

■ Have students continue to write rhythmic units, expanding until they are writing more complex works that require increasingly sophisticated stylistic decision-making and collaborative creativity.

STANDARD 4A

Composing and arranging music within specified guidelines: *Students compose music in several distinct styles, demonstrating creativity in using the elements of music for expressive effect.*

Objective

- Students will compose a rondo by completing a rondo theme together and then working in small groups to compose episodes or contrasting sections.

Materials

- Recording of Wolfgang Amadeus Mozart's *Eine kleine Nachtmusik,* Rondo (fourth movement)
- Small pieces of paper
- Hat
- Chalkboard
- Manuscript paper
- Audio-playback equipment

Prior Knowledge and Experiences

- Students have basic theory skills.
- Students have basic music reading and writing skills.
- Students have studied what a rondo is and have noted instances of repeated design in shapes and colors around them.

Procedures

1. Tell students they are going to compose a rondo. On slips of paper, have students write the names of famous people or places, and have them drop the slips into a hat at the front of the room. Have one student draw a slip out of the hat, and explain that the rhythm of the name or place drawn will be the rhythmic motive of the theme for the class rondo. Read the name on the slip aloud and then have students say it over and over; for example, "Leonardo da Vinci, Leonardo da Vinci. . ." or "Providence, Rhode Island. . . ." Then have them repeat part of the name to create a rhythmic motive; for example, "da Vinci, da Vinci. . . ."

2. Write the letter names of the notes ("A," "B," etc.) on slips of paper and put them into a hat. Then have a student draw several note names, which will be used for the theme of the class rondo. Using these pitches (repeating or altering with accidentals if desired) and the given rhythmic motive, write part of an antecedent phrase on the chalkboard, explaining to students that the antecedent phrase in a rondo asks a question. Then, with students, decide how to complete the antecedent phrase and how to write the consequent phrase—the answer to the question.

3. Explain to students that episodes are musical sections that contrast with the theme. Tell them that each episode must use rhythmic and melodic ideas from the rondo theme and that its ending must lead naturally to the beginning of the rondo theme. Have students work in small groups to write episodes for the rondo—each group will write one—while you circulate to assist them.

4. As students finish writing their episodes, play the developing rondo on the keyboard. Ask those who finish first to write an introduction or a coda.

5. Play a short excerpt of Mozart's *Eine kleine Nachtmusik,* Rondo, and ask students to tap the rhythmic motive on their desk, noting how many times they hear the theme. Tell them to be ready to describe what is similar and what is different between the theme statements and the episodes.

6. Have students discuss Mozart's rondo. Replay the recording as needed to check their ideas. Make sure students recognize the two parts to the theme—the antecedent and consequent phrases—and that the episodes contrast with the theme but use motives from it. Then have students compare their rondo with Mozart's.

7. Tell students to listen to each other's episodes and to point out compositional devices, such as repetition and sequence, that work well. When the rondo is finished, have a student perform it on the keyboard for the class.

Indicators of Success

- Students complete a rondo theme together.

- Students write episodes that relate rhythmically and melodically to their rondo theme.

- Students identify antecedent and consequent phrases and similarities and differences between the theme statements and episodes in Mozart's rondo.

Follow-up

- Have students write compositions in either ABA or rondo form for voice or for instruments they play. Give them the option of adding a synthesizer percussion accompaniment to create a contemporary arrangement.

Composing and arranging music within specified guidelines: *Students compose music in several distinct styles, demonstrating creativity in using the elements of music for expressive effect.*

Objective

- Students will compose a score to accompany a one-minute videotaped segment.

Materials

- Videotape of a movie
- Videocassette recorder
- Video monitor
- Stopwatch
- Manuscript paper
- Keyboard
- Percussion and classroom instruments
- String and wind instruments (optional)

Prior Knowledge and Experiences

- Students have studied music theory.

Procedures

1. Discuss with students the role of music in television and the movies. Ask students to think about the music that might accompany a sunrise scene or a chase scene and to give some examples of scenes where the music plays a major part.

2. Show students a one-minute segment of the selected videotape without sound. Then discuss with them the kind of melody that would fit the scene.

3. Show the segment again and use a stopwatch to time specific events on the screen.

4. Have students work in small groups or alone to write a melody to accompany the videotape. If they do not have notation skills, have them use graphic notation to represent chord clusters, glissandi, or percussion sounds. Suggest that students who play instruments other than the keyboard write for those instruments. Circulate to assist them.

5. Have students perform their sound scores along with the muted videotape. Encourage students to share their reactions to the scores and to note the compositional devices that are especially effective as well as areas that need improvement or that do not add to the action of the scene.

6. Have students make adjustments to their scores and play them a final time for the class with the videotape.

Indicators of Success

- Students create scores that enhance the message of the videotape and that are appropriate for the instruments as well as events on the videotape.

Follow-up

- Have students write other scores; for example, one with two or more parts or one to accompany a short puppet show.

STANDARD 4A
STRATEGY 4 OF 4

Composing and arranging music within specified guidelines: Students compose music in several distinct styles, demonstrating creativity in using the elements of music for expressive effect.

Objective

■ Students will compose a song for solo voice and piano, demonstrating creativity in using the elements of music.

Materials

■ Chalkboard

■ Keyboard (optional for students)

■ String and wind instruments (optional)

■ Manuscript paper

Prior Knowledge and Experiences

■ Students have basic music reading and writing skills.

■ Students have basic theory skills.

■ Students have basic performance skills in voice or on an instrument.

■ Students have selected a person (historical figure, hero), a group of people (the homeless, scouts), an event, or a situation (graduation, loneliness) from the newspaper or a magazine to be the subject of a song they will write.

Procedures

1. Have one student write his or her poem on the chalkboard. Ask everyone to chant the poem several times with a pronounced beat. Then have students clap the rhythm to determine which syllables are accented. Mark those syllables and have students notice the pattern of accented and unaccented beats and determine the bar lines and the meter.

2. Have students then determine the meter of their own poems. Discuss with students compositional devices (repetition, contrast, sequence) and musical structure (phrases, cadences). Have them look for hints in the words of the poem that may help determine the melody; for example, "rain" may suggest short repeated tones, "sunrise" may suggest a rising melody.

3. Have students begin writing their melodies. Tell them to listen to their melodies frequently as they write them. Play the melodies on the piano for them, sing them with the students, or allow students to play them on their own instruments.

4. Write a sample student melody on the chalkboard. Ask the student whose melody is on the board to write the tonic, dominant, subdominant, or supertonic chords of the melody beside it in the same key. Circle the notes on the strong beats of the melody, and help students determine which chords to use for harmony.

5. Have all students determine the chords they will use for the harmony of their melodies.

6. Have students play or sing their melodies for the class.

Indicators of Success

■ Students create melodies that relate to the lyrics they have written.

■ Students determine appropriate chords to harmonize their melodies.

(continued)

- Each student has written a poem of four lines in which either the first two and the last two or the second and fourth lines rhyme.

Follow-up

- Discuss with students ways of using chords for an accompaniment, such as broken chords and arpeggios. Have them write an additional stanza for their melodies and connect the two stanzas with a bridge.

- Have students embellish their melodies with a countermelody on another instrument or voice. Encourage them to write an ending that uses previous musical ideas and brings the piece to a satisfying close.

Composing and arranging music within specified guidelines: Students arrange pieces for voices or instruments other than those for which the pieces were written in ways that preserve or enhance the expressive effect of the music.

Objective

- Students will arrange for other instruments an adaptation of a Handel bourrée, preserving the expressive effect of the music.

Materials

- Excerpt of piano adaptation of Sonata no. 5, Bourrée for Flute and Figured Bass, fourth movement, by George Frideric Handel (see figure)
- Manuscript paper
- Pairs of instruments similar to those Handel used (two clarinets; oboe and bassoon; violin and viola) that class members play
- Piano, or a recording of the piano adaptation of Sonata no. 5, fourth movement

Prior Knowledge and Experiences

- Students have studied music theory.
- Students have basic music reading and writing skills.
- Students have studied the ranges and other qualities, including transposition, of various instruments.
- Some class members are able to play the instruments to be used in the arrangements.

Procedures

1. Distribute copies of the shortened adaptation of the Bourrée. Ask students to choose a pair of instruments similar to those Handel used, and that class members play, that they would like to use in an arrangement (two clarinets; oboe and bassoon; violin and viola). Play the adaptation of the Bourrée on the piano (or play the recording), telling students to think about problems, if any, the arranger or performer might have using the instruments they have chosen.

2. Discuss the score with students in relation to instruments they have selected for their arrangements, noting possible scoring and playing problems, including transposition. Also review with students their earlier discussion of the recording (see "Prior Knowledge"), including the repetition of motives and sections in the work and the overall effect of the music.

3. Have students write their arrangements for two instruments. Remind them that in the case of problems like octave shifts or notes outside of an instrument's range, they must use their own judgment to find solutions. Circulate and assist them as they write.

4. Have students perform each other's arrangements as everyone listens. Then have students discuss the arrangements.

Indicators of Success

- Students write arrangements of the Bourrée that demonstrate their knowledge of orchestration, including consideration of instrument ranges and timbres and sensitivity to the aesthetic qualities of the original composition.

Follow-up

- Have students write another arrangement of the Bourrée using two dissimilar instruments; for example, trumpet and bassoon; flute and viola; oboe and euphonium. Give them the option of adding percussion to create a contemporary, up-tempo arrangement.

(continued)

- Students have listened to and analyzed Handel's Bourrée, including listening to the layers of sound, the timbre, the repetition of motives and sections, and the overall effect of the music.

Arr. Stephen Roemer

Excerpt of piano adaptation of Handel Bourrée.

STANDARD 4B

Composing and arranging music within specified guidelines: Students arrange pieces for voices or instruments other than those for which the pieces were written in ways that preserve or enhance the expressive effect of the music.

Objective

- Students will arrange the melody of a Bach minuet for electronic keyboard, using different tempi, tonalities, and tone colors.

Materials

- Computers (IBM-compatible with Windows, or Macintosh) with MIDI playback capability (for each student)

- Music notation software, such as *Finale*™ (Eden Prairie, MN: Coda Music Technology)

- Scores for "Minuet in G," from *Clavierbüchlein for Anna Magdalena Bach,* by Johann Sebastian Bach

Prior Knowledge and Experiences

- Students have studied music theory.

- On electronic keyboards, students have transcribed and saved the file of their playing of the first sixteen measures of the melody of "Minuet in G."

- Using the step entry method with music notation software, students can add measures, select key signature and meter, and enter notes.

Procedures

1. Have students use the MIDI playback on the computer to listen to their saved versions of the "Minuet in G" at MM=132 while following the score. Then have them analyze the melody in a class discussion by answering these questions: Considering the rhythm only, how many different measures are there? How many times is the rhythm of the first measure used in the sixteen measures? With that much repetition in the rhythm, how does Bach make this tune so musical and so interesting? What examples of unity and variety do you find in the music?

2. Ask students to use the notation software to transpose the music to G minor, changing the key signature to two flats but keeping the notes on the same staff lines and spaces. Then have them listen to the "Minuet" in G minor and describe the effect of the change of modality. Ask them whether any notes sound different from what they expected. This should stimulate a discussion of the concept of the "leading tone." Have students sharp all the F's, listen again, and describe that effect.

3. Have students change the tempo to MM=72, listen again, and compare the effect of the music to the original.

4. Have students use the software to arrange their own variations on Bach's "Minuet" by changing the rhythm. Tell them they may use either the minor version or the original major version that they saved. Encourage students to alter the note values (by using sixteenth notes or triplets, for example) without changing either the pitches or the meter.

5. Have students experiment with new tempi and instrumental colors for their variations.

6. Ask students to perform their variations for the other students. Have the listeners offer feedback about the unity and variety they heard and the aesthetic effect.

7. Have students print and save their arrangements.

(continued)

Indicators of Success

- Using notation software, students create their own arrangements of the melody of the "Minuet in G" with new rhythms, tempi, and tone colors.

- Students evaluate their arrangements on the basis of unity, variety, and aesthetic effect.

Follow-up

- Have students add articulation and dynamic markings to their scores, save them as MIDI files, and import them into a sequencing program for more options (tempi, dynamics, orchestration) for expressive playback.

- Have students create a class work called "Theme and Variations on a Melody by Bach."

Proficient

STANDARD 4C

Composing and arranging music within specified guidelines: Students compose and arrange music for voices and various acoustic and electronic instruments, demonstrating knowledge of the ranges and traditional usages of the sound sources.

Objective

- Students will use synthesized sounds to create a programmatic composition describing one of their classes.

Materials

- Synthesizers
- Audio-playback equipment
- Amplification equipment
- Three sound bites from music in which various musical elements are used in a descriptive fashion, such as Ludwig van Beethoven's Symphony no. 6; Aaron Copland's *Rodeo;* George Gershwin's "An American in Paris"; Kitaro's "Silk Road Fantasy," from *Best of Kitaro* (Kuckuck Music/Celestial Harmonies LC2099); or Yanni's "After the Sunrise," from *Out of Silence* (Private Music/BMG Publishing 2024-2-P)

Prior Knowledge and Experiences

- Students have studied the elements of music.
- Students understand ABA form and its variations.
- Some students have studied synthesizers, sound modules, four-track recorders, microphones, and digital delays.

Procedures

1. Have students listen to one of the three selected sound bites. Ask them to write down, while they listen, what the music brings to mind (for example, a scene, a feeling, an action) and which elements of the music caused them to think that way.

2. Have students share their ideas with each other to see whether a common thread appears in their thoughts. Do the same with the other sound bites.

3. Have students list the subjects and activities that occur in a school day.

4. Review with students ABA form and its variations. Then have groups of two or three students work at synthesizers to compose thirty- to sixty-second compositions in ABA form that describe one of those classes or events.

5. Have each group play its composition for the class, asking students in the other groups to try to ascertain which subject or activity is being described and to explain which elements in the music led to their decision. Then have students who composed the sound bite explain what they were thinking.

6. Have groups consider the responses and make adjustments to their pieces.

Indicators of Success

- Students compose programmatic composition sound bites for synthesizer describing one of their classes.
- Students identify the classes being described and explain how the elements of music are used to create the programmatic sound bites.

Follow-up

- Have students complete a group composition that uses the elements of music in a descriptive fashion to describe an entire school day.

STANDARD 4D

Composing and arranging music within specified guidelines: Students compose music, demonstrating imagination and technical skill in applying the principles of composition.

Objective

- Students will compose music that includes a selected text, using elements of music and various electronic sounds to enhance their compositions.

Materials

- Two short examples of compositions in which various musical elements, including timbre, are used to describe the text (for example, Leonard Bernstein's *West Side Story;* Billy Joel's "Goodnight, Saigon," from *Nylon Curtain,* Columbia 38200; Sergey Prokofiev's *Peter and the Wolf;* or Andrew Lloyd Webber's *The Phantom of the Opera*)

- List of musical elements (on chalkboard)

- Selected six-stanza text ("The wind was on the withered heath . . . and stars were fanned to leaping light") from *The Hobbit,* chapter 7 ("Queer Lodgings"), by J. R. R. Tolkien (New York: Ballantine Books/Random House, 1937)

- Synthesizers and sound sheets

- Audio-playback equipment

- Amplification equipment

- Microphones

Procedures

1. Have students listen to one of the selected pieces of music. Referring to the list of musical elements on the chalkboard, have them listen again while writing down three specific uses of different elements of music that support the text. Have them also list a descriptive word or words to indicate that point in the music. Then discuss with students the music, their selected elements of music, and where those elements occurred in the piece. For example, in *The Phantom of the Opera,* they might say: "repeated rhythmic motif used by bass instruments to set mood"; "minor key used to suggest eerie, dark setting"; or "use of louder dynamics when the Phantom sings his signature line in the song."

2. Have students listen to the other selected piece. Then have them listen again and write down three specific uses of different timbres or sounds that fit well with the text. Tell them to write down a descriptive word or words to indicate that point in the music. Then have students discuss the music and identify their selected timbres or sounds and where they occurred in the music.

3. Have students work in groups of two or three to read the six-stanza text from *The Hobbit.* Ask groups to identify six primary examples of descriptive words similar to the ones found in the two music selections they heard.

4. For each of these six examples, ask students to list the element or elements of music that could best be used to support the text. Then have them use their knowledge of sounds on the synthesizers to list two or three appropriate sounds that could be used for each of the six examples.

5. Distribute the synthesizer sound sheets and have students work in small groups to create compositions that use the identified elements of music and the appropriate sounds to support the provided text, which they will speak into the microphones as part of their compositions. Stop students at various points as they work and have them play portions of their compositions for the rest of the class for discussion and feedback.

6. Have students play their completed compositions for the rest of the class.

(continued)

Prior Knowledge and Experiences

- Students have studied the elements of music.
- Students have studied ABA compositional form and its variations.
- Students have studied programmatic and impressionistic music.
- Students have studied synthesizers, MIDI, four-track recorders, and microphones.
- Some students have studied computer sequencers, sound modules, and digital delays.

Indicators of Success

- Students identify uses of musical elements and sounds in two music examples.
- Students complete a small-group composition using elements of music and various electronic sounds to fit a text from *The Hobbit*.

Follow-up

- Have students select one of the small-group compositions to be presented at the next concert for parents, teachers, and students.

STANDARD 5A

Reading and notating music: Students demonstrate the ability to read an instrumental or vocal score of up to four staves by describing how the elements of music are used.

Objective

- Students will follow a choral score of four staves while listening to a recorded performance and use the score as a basis for describing important aural events in the performance.

Material

- Choral octavos of a selection to be performed in an upcoming concert by the high school choir

- Recording of selection (commercial recording or one made by the school's choir)

- Audio-playback equipment

Prior Knowledge and Experiences

- Students can identify the voice parts (soprano, alto, tenor, bass).

- Student have studied the elements of music and understand homophonic and polyphonic textures.

- Students understand the term "cadence."

Procedures

1. Tell students that the piece they are going to hear is being rehearsed by the school choir for performance. Discuss with them the fact that audiences often enjoy performances more if they are familiar with the music being performed.

2. Give a brief introduction to the score for the choral octavo, pointing out four staves to be read collectively as a system and the rehearsal numbers.

3. Tell students to follow the score as they listen to a recording of the performance, noting important events in the music. While you play the recording, call out the rehearsal numbers to assist novice readers in following the score.

4. Lead a discussion identifying the important events in the piece. Help students identify the primary sections of the piece; the changes in texture, dynamics, and tonality or mode; the thematic exchange among voices; and the thematic variation and development. Replay excerpts to illustrate events as appropriate.

5. Play the recording again, encouraging students to note the important events, such as cadences, as they follow the score.

Indicators of Success

- Students follow the four-part score and describe important aural events, noting how the elements of music are used.

Follow-up

- Provide students with scores of one piece on the concert program so that they can follow the score while listening to the performance.

STANDARD 5C

*Reading and notating music: Students demonstrate the ability to read
a full instrumental or vocal score by describing how the elements
of music are used and explaining all transpositions and clefs.*

Objective

- Students will follow a full instrumental score while listening to a recorded performance and use the score as a basis for describing important aural events in the performance and explaining all transpositions and clefs.

Material

- Conductor's score of a selection to be performed in an upcoming concert by the high school band or orchestra
- Recording of selection (commercial recording or one made by the school's ensemble)
- Audio-playback equipment
- Opaque projector

Prior Knowledge and Experiences

- Students can identify orchestral instruments by sound and names.
- Student have studied the elements of music and understand homophonic and polyphonic textures.
- Students understand the term "cadence."

Procedures

1. Explain to students that the piece they are going to hear is being rehearsed by the band or orchestra for performance. Discuss with them the fact that audiences often enjoy performances more if they are familiar with the music being performed.

2. Place the score on the opaque projector and briefly introduce students to the score. Highlight the rehearsal numbers and the sections that indicate thematic areas. Give students an overview of clefs and transpositions by pointing out the clef and key signature for each instument. Then lead the students as they determine the "keytone" (tonic) for each instrument as well as the concert pitch letter-name of the first note played by each.

3. Instruct students to follow the score as they listen to a recording of the performance, noting important events in the music and the identified thematic areas. While you play the recording, call out occasional rehearsal numbers to assist readers in following the score.

4. Lead a discussion identifying important events, such as the primary sections of the piece; the changes in texture, dynamics, and tonality or mode; the thematic exchange among instruments; and the thematic variation and development of the piece. Replay certain excerpts to illustrate events as appropriate.

5. Play the recording again, encouraging students to note the important events, such as cadences, as they follow the score.

Indicators of Success

- Students follow the score while listening, turning pages at appropriate times.
- Students identify specific events in the music, including primary sections of the piece; the changes in texture, dynamics, and tonality or mode; the thematic exchange among instruments; and the thematic variation and development.
- Students distinguish those instruments that are scored at concert pitch and those that are transposing instruments, and transpose notated pitch names to concert pitch.

(continued)

Follow-up

- Provide students with scores of one piece on the concert program so that they can follow the score while listening to the performance.

- Encourage students to create their own score, using nontraditional notation, as they listen to a favorite recording.

STANDARD 6A

Listening to, analyzing, and describing music: *Students analyze aural examples of a varied repertoire of music, representing diverse genres and cultures, by describing the uses of elements of music and expressive devices.*

Objective

- Students will identify aurally and describe even and uneven rhythmic subdivisions in two different musical selections (or in a traditional march versus a more contemporary march).

Materials

- Recording of "Stars and Stripes Forever" by John Philip Sousa, or another Sousa march in 2/4 meter
- Recording of "The Imperial March" by John Williams, from *Star Wars*
- Audio-playback equipment
- Transparency with selected rhythmic patterns (see steps 2–4)
- Overhead projector
- Nonpitched percussion instruments

Prior Knowledge and Experiences

- Students are able to keep a steady beat.
- Students are familiar with quarter, eighth, and sixteenth notes and the function of the dot in dotted notes.

Procedures

1. Play the recording of the Sousa march while leading students in clapping the beat and then divisions and subdivisions of that beat (quarter, eighth, and sixteenth notes).

2. Divide students into groups, assigning each group one of the following rhythmic patterns:

Select one student to be the conductor. Start the recording and have the conductor signal one of the groups to begin clapping its assigned pattern. Have the conductor make "musical decisions" about when to signal other groups to begin or stop clapping their assigned patterns.

3. Play an excerpt (about one minute) of "The Imperial March," directing students to listen for the predominant rhythms. Discuss with students whether these rhythms are the same as they have been clapping or different, and establish that the predominant rhythmic patterns in "The Imperial March" are more irregular or uneven. Show the transparency with the following rhythms, and lead class in clapping these rhythms, first alone and then with the excerpts from the recording.

(continued)

4. Show students the following notation, and lead them in clapping the upper part first and then the lower part.

5. When students are comfortable with the rhythms, have them clap, one part at a time, along with the recording. Then divide students into small groups so there will be two or three students on each of the two parts in each group. Give groups some time to practice the rhythms using nonpitched percussion instruments.

6. Ask each small group to perform for the class.

Indicators of Success

- Students identify aurally and describe even and uneven subdivisions in two different marches.

- Students explain the function of dotted notes and clap rhythmic patterns at a steady beat when performing in a small group and while listening to a recording.

Follow-up

- Have students listen to music in other meters—for example, 3/4 or 6/8—and follow steps similar to those in Procedures.

- Use a similar process to teach rhythmic patterns using triplets and syncopation.

STANDARD 6A

Listening to, analyzing, and describing music: Students analyze aural examples of a varied repertoire of music, representing diverse genres and cultures, by describing the uses of elements of music and expressive devices.

Objective

- Students will identify tonic and dominant triads by singing them and improvising on resonator bells after listening to excerpts of an opera that uses this harmony.

Materials

- Recording of *La Traviata*, Act III, no. 16 (the letter scene), by Giuseppe Verdi
- Two sets of resonator bells (or two xylophones)
- Chalkboard
- Paper
- Audio-playback equipment

Prior Knowledge and Experiences

- Students have some experience in part singing.
- Students have studied solfège and the Kodály hand signs.
- Students have some experience with vocal improvisation.

Procedures

1. Have students make three columns on a sheet of paper. Direct them to place a mark in the first column representing the first chord they hear in the musical excerpt for the lesson. Tell them they should place a mark in the second column when the chord changes. Then, if the next chord change returns to the first chord, they should place a mark in the first column; if it is a different chord, they should place a mark in the third column. Explain that they should continue marking the chord changes in this manner throughout the excerpt.

2. Play an excerpt from Act III, no. 16, of *La Traviata,* directing students to listen for chord changes and mark them as directed in step 1. Following the listening experience, lead a discussion helping students discover that there were two chords. Have them label the first column "I" and the second column "V."

3. Play the excerpt again, directing students to identify the solfège names for the roots of the chords (*do* and *sol*). Then play the entire recording of Act III, no. 16, directing students to show "home chords" (tonic) by holding hands close to body and "away chords" (dominant) by extending arms full length.

4. Tell students that A♭ is the tonal center and guide them in spelling tonic and dominant chords in this key. Notate the chords on the board as students spell them.

5. Assign vocal parts to students and chord pitches to the parts. Notate these on the chalkboard as in the following example:

Tonic (I)		Dominant (V)	
Bass	*do* (A♭)	Bass	*sol* (E♭)
Tenor	*mi* (C)	Tenor	*re* (B♭)
Alto	*sol* (E♭)	Alto	*sol* (E♭)
Soprano	*do* (A♭)	Soprano	*ti* (G)

6. Lead students in singing the two chords until they can do so with ease.

7. Play the recording again, directing students to sing softly their assigned pitches with the chords on the recording as you or a student points to the chords on the board.

(continued)

8. Give one student resonator bells for the I chord and another the bells for the V chord. Lead class in singing the chord progression I-I-V-V-I-I-V-V-I-I, etc. (four beats per chord), as students improvise with bells on the appropriate chord. Then have students form two lines—one behind each set of bells—and have each student improvise two four-beat patterns on the bells, while all students sing. After improvising two four-beat patterns, each student goes to the end of the other line to play the other chord.

Indicators of Success

- Students identify aurally the tonic and dominant chords in Verdi's *La Traviata*, Act III, no. 16.

- Students sustain their parts in singing the tonic-dominant chord progression.

- Students improvise rhythms, using resonator bells or xylophones, within the appropriate harmonic context.

Follow-up

- Provide recordings of some simple folk songs (using only two or three different chords) and have students "chart" chord changes using the three-column recording procedure introduced in steps 1 and 2.

- Have students listen to current popular music and identify chord changes—not necessarily naming chords, but noting when the harmony changes.

STANDARD 6B

Listening to, analyzing, and describing music: Students demonstrate extensive knowledge of the technical vocabulary of music.

Objective

- Students will identify aurally cadences in music and describe their importance to the structure and expressiveness of a composition.

Material

- Recording of "Tuba Mirum," from *Requiem,* by Wolfgang Amadeus Mozart
- Score for "Tuba Mirum"
- Audio-playback equipment
- Chalkboard

Prior Knowledge and Experiences

- Students have studied the meaning of cadences, have heard them played in keyboard demonstrations, and have identified them in recorded excerpts.

Procedures

1. Review various types of cadences (authentic, full, half, deceptive) with students by playing a variety of them on the keyboard and having students identify them, by reviewing the definitions of the various cadences, and by writing out several examples on the chalkboard.

2. Distribute copies of the score for "Tuba Mirum," and review with students the techniques for following a score, including identifying the staves assigned to the various voice parts and the accompaniment, rehearsal numbers (or letters), and dynamic and tempo markings.

3. Play the recording of "Tuba Mirum," having students follow the score and note measures in which they identify cadences.

4. Lead a discussion through which students identify (a) cadences that conclude major sections of the piece, marking the end of one feeling and making way for the introduction of a new one; (b) cadences that help build expectation and tension; and (c) cadences that help resolve tension, coming to a point of rest. Replay excerpts of the recording to illustrate.

5. Play the recording a final time, having students raise their hands when the cadences occur.

Indicators of Success

- Students demonstrate their ability to identify cadences by raising their hands when the cadences occur in the music.
- Students describe the importance of cadences to the structure and expressiveness of a composition, using specific examples.

Follow-up

- Have students listen to recordings of their choice and identify the cadences.
- Have students improvise compositions, carefully planning cadences within the composition.

Listening to, analyzing, and describing music: Students identify and explain compositional devices and techniques used to provide unity and variety and tension and release in a musical work and give examples of other works that make similar uses of these devices and techniques.

Objective

- Students describe the compositional structure, including the use of unity and variety and of tension and release in a symphony.

Materials

- *Antonin Dvorak, Symphony #9*, CD-ROM, by Robert Winter (New York: Voyager)
- Computers with CD-ROM capabilities

Prior Knowledge and Experiences

- Students have worked with CD-ROM programs.
- Students have developed a vocabulary for describing music.
- Students have some experience in analytical listening to symphonic masterworks.

Procedures

1. Provide a general overview of the symphony as a musical form, emphasizing that it is a work in four movements with contrasting tempo, tonal centers, and thematic material, yet unified by "program," tonal relationships, and sometimes, thematic relationships.

2. Provide a general introduction to the Dvorak CD-ROM, showing students the section titled "A Pocket Guide." Guide their overview by pointing out that (a) each column of the guide represents one of the symphony's four movements and that (b) the words in each column describe the sequence of events within each movement (for example, the first movement has an introduction, a section called "exposition with a first theme, a transition, and a second theme," etc.). Demonstrate to students how they can hear any portion of this symphony by moving the cursor to the words that identify the section and "clicking" on that section.

3. Assign students, either individually, or in small groups, to complete the subprogram for the first movement, "A Close Reading," twice, following the on-screen commentary as they listen the first time, and following the on-screen highlighted score the second time.

4. After all students have completed the subprogram, lead a class discussion on such questions as:

   How does the primary theme differ from the secondary theme?

   How do the two themes differ structurally?

   Do the two themes convey similar or contrasting feelings?

   Do the transition sections serve to build or release tension? How does the musical structure enable them to do this?

   Is the development section one of high tension, low tension, or changing tension?

   Does the coda build or release tension? How is this accomplished musically?

   Use the "Pocket Guide" as a basis for this discussion, replaying sections of the music frequently to verify the discussion.

Indicators of Success

■ Through discussions, students demonstrate their ability to describe the structure of the work using appropriate musical terms, such as exposition, development, recapitulation, main theme, and transition.

■ Through discussions, students demonstrate awareness of points of tension and release within the composition and of the musical devices (ascending melody, elongated rhythm, thickening texture, etc.) that created them.

Follow-up

■ Have students identify major structural components in a recording of the first movement of a Mozart symphony.

■ Encourage students to explore other aspects of the program—the Dvorak biography, "New World Listening," and the "Getting to Carnegie Hall" game.

■ Provide students with additional CD-ROM music analysis programs to guide their listening.

■ Encourage students to design listening guides for other recordings, using a format similar to the one in the Dvorak CD-ROM program.

Listening to, analyzing, and describing music: Students identify and explain compositional devices and techniques used to provide unity and variety and tension and release in a musical work and give examples of other works that make similar uses of these devices and techniques.

Objective

- Students will identify sequences in a recording of Native American music and explain how sequences unify the piece as well as provide variety.

Materials

- Recording of "Butterfly Dance" (Native American music of the San Juan Pueblo Indians), which accompanies *The World of Music,* 3rd ed., by David Willoughby (Madison, WI: Brown & Benchmark Publishers, 1996)

- Printed music for a keyboard piece that contains sequences (see step 1), such as "Minuet in G Major" by Johann Sebastian Bach, from *Notebook for Anna Magdalene*

- Song that contains sequences (see step 1), such as "Music Alone Shall Live," in *The Music Connection,* Grade 4, teacher's edition only (Parsippany, NJ: Silver Burdett Ginn, 1995); *Share the Music,* Grade 4 (New York: Macmillan/McGraw-Hill, 1995); or *World of Music,* Grades 4 and 5 (Parsippany, NJ: Silver Burdett Ginn, 1991)

- Audio-playback equipment

- Opaque projector

Procedures

1. As a review, play a piece with sequences on the keyboard, show students the notation using an opaque projector, and ask students to identify the sequences aurally and visually. Then sing a song that contains sequences. Have students locate the sequences aurally and by finding them in the notation.

2. Play the recording of "Butterfly Dance," directing students to listen for and identify sequences.

3. Lead a brief discussion with students on the location of sequences in this piece. Ask them to describe the way the sequences provide repetition of musical ideas while introducing variety. Discuss with them how sequences build tension.

4. Play the recording of "Butterfly Dance" once again as students listen. Encourage them to pay special attention to the unity and variety and the building of tension created by the sequences.

Indicators of Success

- Students identify sequences in the recording.

- Students describe how sequences provide unity and variety and build tension in the piece.

Follow-up

- Have students improvise on a keyboard or mallet instrument a short melody that includes sequences.

- Send students on a "sequence search," reviewing all of the songs sung in class and identifying any melodic sequences those pieces might contain.

(continued)

■ Opaque projector

Prior Knowledge and Experiences

■ Students have had experience identifying sequences in a number of compositions that they have performed or heard.

STANDARD 6E

Listening to, analyzing, and describing music: Students compare ways in which musical materials are used in a given example relative to ways in which they are used in other works of the same genre or style.

Objective

- Students will identify and describe uses of vocal style, melodic form, and accompaniment upon hearing aural examples of various Native American songs.

Materials

- CD and book set *Creation's Journey,* Smithsonian Folkways, SF 40410
- Audio-playback equipment
- Paper
- Chalkboard

Prior Knowledge and Experiences

- Students have studied distinguishing vocal and stylistic characteristics of a variety of regional and tribal styles.

Procedures

1. Direct students' attention to the following list of questions on the chalkboard: Are the singers male, female, or mixed? Describe the sound/style of singing (for example, nasal, tense, relaxed). Is the form AB, ABA, call-and-response, or other? What type of instruments, if any, are used in the example? Describe the rhythms in the melody and accompaniment.

2. Tell students to think about these questions as they listen to the music and to take notes based on the questions for a later question-and-answer discussion.

3. Play recordings of "Prairie Chicken Dance," "Hello Song," and "Axawiri Imilla" from *Creation's Journey,* directing students to complete their answer sheets while they listen.

4. After the listenings, discuss each example with the students. Ask student volunteers to describe each selection by answering the questions on the board. Answers should include the following:

   "Prairie Chicken Dance": male voices; high, tense, falsetto; melody starts high and gradually descends; solo singer initiates song with group entering and all singing to end of song; drum beats in accompaniment use accents and dynamics to mark dance movements.

   "Hello Song": mixed male and female voices; mostly unison; alternation between singing and recitative; diverse drum rhythms in accompaniment with many starts and stops.

   "Axawiri Imilla": alternating male and female voices with occasional use of mixed voices; voices high, thin, bright, and nasal; rapid tempo; a capella; call-and-response form.

5. Discuss the conclusions of the volunteers with the class until all the questions have been answered correctly. Then have students draw conclusions about vocal style, melodic form, and accompaniment in Native American music. Have students listen to the three selections again, following the correct answers on the board.

Indicators of Success

- Students recognize and describe distinguishing characteristics of each example during a class discussion, and they recognize these as characteristics of Native American music.

Follow-up

- Repeat the strategy using music from another culture—African, Asian, South American. Then have students compare and contrast the music of that culture with Native American music.

STANDARD 6F

Advanced

Listening to, analyzing, and describing music: Students analyze and describe uses of the elements of music in a given work that make it unique, interesting, and expressive.

Objective

- Students analyze and describe the musical structure of the Japanese musical form gagaku and compare its structure to that of traditional Western orchestral music.

Material

- Recording of "Entenraku," from *Gagaku: Imperial Court Music of Japan,* Lyrichord (LLST 7126); or *The Music Connection,* Grade 6 (Parsippany, NJ: Silver Burdett Ginn, 1995)
- Audio-playback equipment
- Manuscript paper

Prior Knowledge and Experiences

- Students have studied the background of gagaku, a form of Japanese court music.
- Students have considered the effect of the basic axiom of the Japanese arts ("Maximum effect from minimum material") on the design of Japanese temples, shrines, woodcuts, and flower arrangements.
- Students have studied the structure of traditional Western orchestral music.

Procedures

1. Have students listen to the first section of "Entenraku" and decide whether the texture is thick or thin and how the musical texture compares with the economy of means practiced in the visual arts they have previously studied. Explain to students that the Japanese value each sound as a single thread in a fine tapestry; the sounds are limited so that the listener can carefully follow each strand.

2. Ask students to listen again and be ready to describe the timbres that create the texture of "Entenraku": oboe (Japanese: *hichirichi*), mouth organ (Japanese: *sho*), strings (Japanese: koto and *biwa*), and drums (*kakko* [small drum] and *taiko* [large drum]).

3. Discuss with students the heterophonic structure of "Entenraku," helping them to hear that a melody is played in one voice while a variation is played simultaneously in another voice. Point out to students that at times, the melodic lines shift ahead and behind one another in a "sliding door" effect, and that rather than playing the entire melody, some instruments play only the "essential tones," providing a basic outline or abbreviation of the melody.

4. Explain to students that gagaku uses a breath rhythm, which might be compared to a rubato or ritard played by a Western string quartet. Demonstrate by playing an excerpt with a breath rhythm in "Entenraku." Then have students conduct in 4/4 and follow the breath rhythm by lengthening the fourth beat. Help them to hear the great tension this creates as it leads to the following beat. Explain to students that one of the thrills of gagaku is watching the drummer's hands rise high in the air in anticipation of the next beat.

5. Ask each student to select an instrument in the piece and play its pattern with fingers on the desk, noting whether it marks off beats or large sections (small drum keeps the beat; large drum marks off larger sections; strings also perform percussive functions, with arpeggios marking larger sections). Help them to hear the interlocking ostinatos that provide the basic time organization.

6. Have students sing the melody and notate the pentatonic scale: E-(F#)-G-A-B-(C)-D-E. Explain that F# and C are auxiliary tones in this scale, which is called the Ritsu mode, a mode used in Chinese and Korean music.

7. Have students compare the structure of gagaku music with the structure of Western orchestral music. Although both use woodwinds, strings, and percussion, in gagaku, high-pitched winds are prominent as melody instruments, and strings often serve a percussive function; in the Western orchestra, strings are often the melody instruments. In gagaku, the preferred texture is much thinner than that of the Western orchestra, and the emphasis is on individual timbres and lines, making the structure horizontal and heterophonic rather than vertical and chordal.

Indicators of Success

- Students describe the structure of gagaku music and compare it with that of the Western orchestra.

Follow-up

- Assign students to create a short multimedia production that includes "Entenraku," drummer movements determined by breath rhythms, Japanese woodcuts, and Japanese flower arrangements.

Evaluating music and music performances: Students evolve specific criteria for making informed, critical evaluations of the quality and effectiveness of performances, compositions, arrangements, and improvisations and apply the criteria in their personal participation in music.

Objective

- Students will develop a list of at least five components of a quality musical composition.

Materials

- Recordings, supplied by students
- Audio-playback equipment for each group of students
- Chalkboard
- Paper

Prior Knowledge and Experiences

- Students have had experience analyzing and discussing music.
- Students have identified recordings that they consider to be examples of quality music.

Procedures

1. Divide class into small groups, assigning in each group one student to be the discussion leader, one to be the recorder, and one to be the audio technician.

2. Ask students to develop a list of at least five criteria that make music "good." Stress the fact that this assignment is concerned with the composition of music and not the quality of the performance. Allow students to listen to excerpts of recordings they have brought in to help them in developing their lists, but tell them that no single recording should be played for more than one minute. Give the groups time to work, circulating among them to keep them on task and to offer suggestions.

3. Reassemble the class and play a brief excerpt of two to three recordings as recorders from each group list their group's criteria on the chalkboard.

4. Discuss with students whether the criteria they have developed are valid for labeling "good" music. Replay excerpts of students' recordings frequently to validate the criteria, which might include the following: interesting sound and combinations of sound, repetition of patterns with subtle and interesting variations, contrasting (but related) patterns, balance, style consistency, conveys a feeling.

5. Work with students to create a master list of criteria on the chalkboard.

Indicators of Success

- Students identify and discuss the components of music that contribute to quality compositions.

Follow-up

- Invite the art teacher to visit the class and discuss what makes a good painting. Have students compare the criteria used in evaluating art with those used in evaluating music.
- Assign students to interview musicians in the community (for example, church organist, music store owner, community band director, radio station DJ), getting wider views on what makes good music.

STANDARD 7A

Evaluating music and music performances: Students evolve specific criteria for making informed, critical evaluations of the quality and effectiveness of performances, compositions, arrangements, and improvisations and apply the criteria in their personal participation in music.

Objective

- Students will develop lists of criteria that might be employed by professional music critics in evaluating compositions and performances and apply these criteria as they listen critically themselves.

Materials

- Copies (for each group) of four or five reviews of performances from the *New York Times* and of new recordings from *Hi-Fi Review, Rolling Stone,* or similar sources
- One of the recordings reviewed
- Audio-playback equipment
- Paper
- Chalkboard

Prior Knowledge and Experiences

- Students are familiar with the role of the music critic—to listen carefully to music and music performances and to offer an "expert opinion" on the value of the music, performances, recordings, and so on.

Procedures

1. Divide class into groups of three to five students, assigning in each group one student to be the discussion leader and one to be the recorder. Tell each group to find space to work independently.

2. Distribute copies of the reviews and tell students to carefully read these reviews written by professional music critics and to list the things the music critics considered important in making their evaluations. Give groups time to work, circulating among them to keep them on task and to offer suggestions.

3. Reassemble the class and ask if there was any terminology they did not understand in the reviews. Help them to understand those terms and then play an excerpt of a recording critiqued in one of the reviews.

4. Have recorders from each group list their group's criteria on the chalkboard. Discuss with the class the criteria they listed, frequently replaying excerpts from the recording to illustrate certain aspects of it and to illustrate application of the criteria.

5. Create one master list on the chalkboard that covers what all the reviewers felt was important in good music.

Indicators of Success

- Students develop a master list of evaluative criteria used by music critics in the selected reviews.
- Students apply criteria from their list in their critical listening of the selected recording.

Follow-up

- Have students use the master criteria list derived from the reviews as a basis for writing their own critiques of a "live" or televised concert or a recording.

STANDARD 7B

Evaluating music and music performances: Students evaluate a performance, composition, arrangement, or improvisation by comparing it to similar or exemplary models.

Objective

- Students will critically evaluate a recorded performance of a school ensemble compared with a recorded version of a professional ensemble performing the same composition.

Materials

- Concert recording of the school band or choir playing a selected composition
- Professional recording of the same composition
- Audio-playback equipment

Prior Knowledge and Experiences

- Students have developed critical listening skills.
- Students have developed a basic vocabulary for discussing the elements of music.
- Students have established criteria for evaluating music performances.

Procedures

1. Divide students into groups of four to six students, assigning a discussion leader and a recorder in each group. Give groups the task of listing features that distinguish a "good" performance from a "great" performance. Point out that the focus is not on what is performed but on the way in which it is performed.

2. Reassemble students after ten minutes. Work with them to compile a master list of distinguishing features.

3. Have students listen to the two recordings of the same composition and, using their criteria, have them decide what makes the professional performance "great." (If the composition is more than three minutes, use only an excerpt from each.) Be sure students identify the special features and the absence or presence of these features in the performances.

4. Lead a discussion in which students explain how they applied the criteria they developed to the two performances. Have students listen to the two performances again, noting the established criteria.

Indicators of Success

- Students list features that distinguish a "great" performance from a "good" performance.
- Students identify the presence or absence of the distinguishing features in the performances they hear.

Follow-up

- Record (preferably on different days) several versions of a class performance of the same song. At a later date, replay the recordings and lead a discussion in which students critically compare the performances.

STANDARD 7C

Evaluating music and music performances: Students evaluate a given musical work in terms of its aesthetic qualities and explain the musical means it uses to evoke feelings and emotions.

Objective

- Students will write a critical review of a new music selection for a newspaper, explaining how the music evokes feelings and emotions.

Materials

- Recording of a new release by an obscure group (perhaps provided by a radio DJ)
- Copies of student-generated evaluative criteria
- Chalkboard

Prior Knowledge and Experiences

- Students have had experiences in critical listening and describing music in appropriate music terminology.
- Students have developed criteria for evaluating compositions, including criteria that cover the following: (a) composition has repeated musical ideas to provide unity, and diverse ideas to provide variety; (b) various sections of the composition are connected in a logical and interesting way; (c) composition is carefully crafted with attention to subtle details such as articulation, dynamic shading, and phrasing; and (d) listener is inwardly moved when experiencing the piece.

Procedures

1. Distribute copies of the evaluative criteria students developed in a previous class. Explain to students that their assignment will be to write a one- or two-paragraph critique of an obscure "pop style" song by a group unknown to the class. Note that the critique should be similar to a listing that a newspaper might publish to help readers decide whether or not to purchase the recording.

2. Discuss with students points that they should keep in mind in writing their critiques and make a list on the chalkboard. The list should include points such as the following: (a) sources of sound (instruments or voices used—timbre); (b) use of musical elements (melody, harmony, rhythm, texture); (c) overall structure (form) of the composition; (d) critique of the music, rather than the way it is performed; (e) comment on the expressiveness of the composition; and (f) critique should reflect an informed judgment about the composition.

3. Play the selected recording several times as students write.

4. Ask several students to read their critiques to the class. Encourage class discussion about each critique, referring to both the evaluative criteria that students have developed and the points they discussed regarding a good critique in step 2.

Indicators of Success

- Students demonstrate in their reviews an awareness of the composition's expressiveness and of the structural elements of music that contributed to that expression.

Follow-up

- Using a tape you assemble with one- to two-minute excerpts of music randomly selected from radio stations, have students evaluate each selection, justifying their judgments with the evaluative criteria they established earlier.
- Select several works by contemporary composers of art music, and have students evaluate each work using the criteria they established.

STANDARD 8A

Understanding relationships between music, the other arts, and disciplines outside the arts:
Students explain how elements, artistic processes, and organizational principles are
used in similar and distinctive ways in the various arts and cite examples.

Objective

- Students will identify repetition as an organizational principle in music, the visual arts, and dance.

Materials

- Recording of Béla Bartók's "Bagatelle," op. 6, no. 3
- Reproduction of painting "Two Miracles of St. Nicholas of Bari" by Fra Angelico
- Photographs or drawings of the five major positions in ballet
- Audio-playback equipment

Prior Knowledge and Experiences

- Students have developed a vocabulary to describe music and other art forms.

Procedures

1. Introduce Bartók's "Bagatelle" by pointing out that composers usually present new musical ideas in a composition as well as find interesting ways to repeat an idea. Play the recording, and then ask students which of the two they found Bartók primarily doing in this composition.

2. Lead a discussion about the repetition found in the Bartók piece. Replay the recording as necessary to help students hear the repetitive use of the melodic cluster and to identify the various ways Bartók found to repeat this idea.

3. Noting that dance also uses repetition, introduce the five positions of ballet using the photographs or drawings. Have students choose a position and take that position through space. (For example, if students choose a particular position for hands and arms, they should retain that position as they move lower toward the floor or higher toward the ceiling. If they choose a position for the feet, they should retain that position for the feet as they move across the room.) Have them change from one position to another. Then have them repeat all five positions in place and then move each position through space.

4. Compare Bartók's repetitive use of the melodic cluster in "Bagatelle" with a ballet dancer repeating a position in one place and moving it through space for contrast.

5. Present the Fra Angelico painting, asking students to study the elements that create repetition; for example, help students to see the lines in the water, which are repeated in the ships.

6. Lead a discussion in which students compare the use of repetition as well as contrast in music, dance, and the visual arts and describe how repetition and contrast are used as a means of providing organization and expression.

Indicators of Success

- Students identify repetition in several art forms and explain how it is used to provide organization.

Follow-up

- Have students listen again to "Bagatelle" and look at Fra Angelico's painting, listening and looking for different organizational principles, such as tension and release, balance and imbalance, and thick and thin textures.

- Using music and paintings from different style periods or cultures, have students identify various organizational principles.

Understanding relationships between music, the other arts, and disciplines outside the arts:
Students explain how elements, artistic processes, and organizational principles are
used in similar and distinctive ways in the various arts and cite examples.

Objective

- Students will identify repeated elements, contrasting elements, and the results of repetition and contrast on the total effect of selected music and visual art works.

Materials

- Picture of a Baroque church interior
- Copies of three Rembrandt paintings, including "The Night Watch" and one or more portraits
- Recording of Johann Sebastian Bach's Toccata in D minor
- Audio-playback equipment

Prior Knowledge and Experiences

- Students are aware that Rembrandt lived from 1606 to 1669 in Holland; and Bach, from 1685 to 1750 in Germany.
- Students have studied the Baroque period in music.

Procedures

1. Have students analyze the picture of the Baroque church, noting the total effect of the interior; for example, Is the interior cold or warm? Help students to discover what qualities convey this total effect. Note the lines, shapes, and colors that provide the means of unity as well as those that provide the means of contrast in the chapel. Then have them speculate on how the church's interior might affect those attending a service there and explain why they feel that way.

2. Have students analyze the Rembrandt paintings, noting the repeated lines, shapes, and colors that create unity as well as the sharp contrasts in the painting. Point out in particular in "The Night Watch" painting the spotlight effect and how it creates a stark contrast.

3. Have students concentrate particularly on the Rembrandt portraits and speculate on the messages Rembrandt was trying to convey. Have them note the lines, shapes, and colors that reinforce the message and help them to explain how they do this.

4. As students listen to the recording of Bach's Toccata in D minor, have them sketch maps of the music as memory aids. Then have them analyze the means of unity (repeated motives; steady, unflagging beat) and the means of contrast (soft and loud; high and low; slow and fast; thick texture of slow block chords and thin texture of rapid, florid passages).

5. Have students compare the sounds in Bach's music with the lines, shapes, and colors of the church interior and discuss the effect of each.

6. Discuss with students the overall effect of Bach's music and the message he seems to communicate and compare that with the effect of Rembrandt's paintings.

7. Have students compare the picture of the church, the paintings, and the music and help them make a list of the characteristics of Baroque music and Baroque painting and architecture.

Indicators of Success

- Students identify repeated and contrasting elements in the selected music and visual art works.

- Students describe the results of repetition and contrast on the total effect of the selected works.

Follow-up

- Have students reexamine the music and paintings on another day. Ask them to describe the feelings of tension and release evoked by the works and the techniques the composer and painter used to create those feelings.

- Have students explore repetition and contrast in other works of art from different style periods and genres.

Understanding relationships between music, the other arts, and disciplines outside the arts:
Students explain how elements, artistic processes, and organizational principles are
used in similar and distinctive ways in the various arts and cite examples.

Objective

- Students will compare the use of repetition and contrast in music, art, and dance.

Materials

- *Music! Its Role and Importance in Our Lives,* by Charles Fowler (New York: Glencoe/McGraw-Hill, 1994)
- Paper

Prior Knowledge and Experiences

- None required

Procedures

1. Ask students to read the section "Orders Based on Repetition," beginning on page 147 through the end of the section on "Order in American Popular Songs" on page 151 in *Music! Its Role and Importance in Our Lives.*

2. Have students sing "My Funny Valentine" (page 149). Point out how they can use the red and blue lines, which identify repeated and contrasting melodic themes, as an aid to their singing. Discuss the changes in each appearance of the A section.

3. Have students divide into small groups of five to seven students, and ask groups to develop "maps" (visual representations) that outline the structure of the piece. Note that the big structural components of the song are eight-measure phrases. Ask students what smaller units of repetition can be found within each phrase.

4. Have each group present its map for class discussion. Then have the class sing the melody again.

5. Ask students to examine the photographs of the Robert Indiana painting "The Figure Five" (page 150) and the U.S. Capitol (page 151) and discuss these questions: What are the large and small structural components in these works of art? Which elements provide repetition? Which provide contrast?

6. Direct students' attention to the photograph of the Alvin Ailey dancers on page 62 of the text. Discuss the following questions with the students: How do the positions of the dancers' feet show repetition? How do they show contrast? How do the positions of the hands show order? How do they show chaos?

7. Have students read "Order in the Cuban Rumba" on pages 151–53 in the text and then perform the percussion part given for a type of rumba called *guaguanco*. Discuss with them ways in which the various rhythm patterns provide repetition and contrast and contribute to an orderly structure for the music.

Indicators of Success

- Students identify and discuss elements that provide repetition and contrast in various works of art.

Follow-up

■ Assign students, individually or in small groups, to select current popular recordings, create maps outlining the structure of some of the songs on these recordings, and create dance movements to reflect the structure of the music.

STANDARD 8B

Understanding relationships between music, the other arts, and disciplines outside the arts: Students compare characteristics of two or more arts within a particular historical period or style and cite examples from various cultures.

Objective

- Students will compare characteristics of Baroque music and visual art, identifying ornamentation as one of the elements that characterize the arts of this period.

Materials

- *Music! Its Role and Importance in Our Lives,* by Charles Fowler (New York: Glencoe/McGraw-Hill, 1994)
- Recording of "Winter" (fourth movement), from *The Four Seasons* by Antonio Vivaldi
- Audio-playback equipment
- Chalkboard

Prior Knowledge and Experiences

- Students have had some experience in listening to, viewing, and using technical terms to describe both music and visual arts.

Procedures

1. Lead students in an examination of the photograph of the altarpiece of San Esteban (page 449 of the text) by the Spanish architect José Benito de Churriguera, comparing it with church altars in your community in terms of size, materials used in construction, shapes, and colors. Emphasize the lavish ornamentation that leads to exaggerated emotional response to this construction.

2. Have students read the definition of "baroque" and the historical context of the Baroque period (pages 448–53). Ask them to verify points in the text by referring to the photograph again.

3. Through discussion, have students speculate on the ways a composer might ornament music. List ideas on the chalkboard.

4. Explain to students that they will be hearing the movement "Winter," from Vivaldi's *The Four Seasons* and that they should compare this work with the list of ways of ornamentation developed in step 3. Play the recording.

5. After listening, discuss the kinds of ornamentation that the students heard in the work.

6. Based on their discussion of the photograph of the San Esteban altarpiece and the Vivaldi recording, have students compare the ornamentation in each work. Discuss how the creators of these works used ornamentation in their works to arouse emotions.

Indicators of Success

- Students identify aspects of ornamentation in the San Esteban altarpiece and the movement "Winter" in *The Four Seasons* and compare in terms of the creators' representation of Baroque style.

Follow-up

- Have students, working individually or in small groups, locate other examples of elaborately ornamented Baroque art (such as paintings, statues, architecture, or costumes) and music.

- Play an excerpt from a recording of an elaborately ornamented Baroque composition and one from another style period. Have students identify the Baroque selection based on the ornamentation.

STANDARD 8C

Proficient

Understanding relationships between music, the other arts, and disciplines outside the arts: Students explain ways in which the principles and subject matter of various disciplines outside the arts are interrelated with those of music.

Objective

- Students will analyze songs of the Civil War era and describe how the beliefs and feelings of the people who first sang them are revealed through both the lyrics and the musical content of the songs.

Materials

- "The Battle Hymn of the Republic" and "Dixie," in *Song Session Community Songbook* (Miami: Warner Bros. Publications, 1995)
- "John Brown's Body," in *Reader's Digest Children's Songbook* (Milwaukee: Hal Leonard Corporation, 1986)

Prior Knowledge and Experiences

- Students have studied in their history classes the issues that caused the Civil War.
- Students are aware that the words for "The Battle Hymn of the Republic" were written by Julia Ward Howe after visiting the Union soldiers at a battle front near Washington, D.C., during the Civil War.

Procedures

1. After reviewing what the song is about, have students sing "The Battle Hymn of the Republic" with an upbeat tempo as you accompany them on the keyboard. Then ask students to analyze the lyrics by picking out words or phrases with a high emotional effect; for example, "The glory of the coming of the Lord," "His truth is marching on," "As He died to make men holy, let us die to make men free," and "Glory, glory Hallelujah!" Have them speculate on the effect these words had on Northerners who sang them and on the effect that religion might have had as a motivator to those engaged in fighting the war.

2. Have students sing the abolitionist song "John Brown's Body" with an upbeat tempo as you accompany them on the keyboard. Explain to them that this song provided the melody for "The Battle Hymn of the Republic." Lead a discussion speculating on the effect "John Brown's Body" may have had on the Northerners who later associated it with "The Battle Hymn of the Republic."

3. Have students analyze the musical content of "The Battle Hymn of the Republic." Consider with them the following: the effect of the 4/4 meter, and how the effect would be different if the song were in 3/4 or 6/8 meter; and the effect of the strong, steady beat and the dotted rhythms, and how that effect would change if the dots were eliminated. Also, consider the melody that forms an arch in measures one through four and five through eight and the effect of the lift in pitch (for example, Does it make the message more tranquil or more triumphant? Does it reinforce the meaning of the words? What would the effect be if the melody dipped down instead of arching upward?). Consider, too, whether any words or melodies repeat, and whether repetition might have had an effect on the popularity of the song.

4. Have students sing "Dixie," the song of the South, and describe what the song is about. Ask them to pick out words that seem especially to reveal the feelings of the person who wrote the song and of those who sang it.

5. Have students analyze the meter, rhythm patterns, shape of the melodic line, and repeated words and melodies in "Dixie." Then have them decide how the music reinforces the message of the words.

(continued)

6. Finally, in a class discussion, ask students to compare the effects of melody and rhythm in "Dixie," "The Battle Hymn of the Republic," and "John Brown's Body" and to reflect on the value of the musical message of the songs and the perspective the messages give to textbook facts.

Indicators of Success

- By analyzing songs from the Civil War, students describe how music can reflect and influence emotions.

- Students describe the value of music in understanding people of other times and places.

Follow-up

- Have students locate examples in other arts that communicate the beliefs and feelings of the Civil War era; for example, paintings, poems, literature, theatre, and the folk arts.

- Have students examine music (and other arts) of other wars (for example, music of World War I or Vietnam), particularly the way in which music deepens the feelings communicated by the texts and helps them to understand the time in history.

STANDARD 8E

Understanding relationships between music, the other arts, and disciplines outside the arts:
Students explain how the roles of creators, performers, and others involved in the production and presentation of the arts are similar to and different from one another in the various arts.

Objective

- Students will identify, describe, and contrast the various jobs necessary to bring a musical theatre production to the stage.

Materials

- Video recording *Broadway Backstage!* (The Midtown Management Group, Inc., 120 West 44th Street, Suite 601, New York, NY 10036; 212-398-6740), 1985
- Videocassette recorder
- Video monitor
- Chalkboard
- Paper

Prior Knowledge and Experiences

- Students have seen videos of Broadway productions or have attended a live performance of a musical by either a professional or an amateur company.

Procedures

1. Discuss with students the importance of teamwork and support personnel to any accomplishment. Help students to think about the fact that school requires not only students and teachers but also administrators, a school board, taxpayers, secretaries, custodians, bus drivers, and so on.

2. Turn the discussion to Broadway shows and guide students in making a preliminary list on the chalkboard of jobs that must be done to bring a production to the stage.

3. Play the videotape "Broadway Backstage!" and instruct students to add on a piece of paper to the list of jobs from the chalkboard as they watch the tape.

4. Have students continue the discussion of jobs, adding the new jobs they noticed in the video and describing them.

5. Divide class into small groups, and assign each group one on-stage and one off-stage job to compare. Give the groups five minutes to discuss their jobs. Then have each group report to the rest of the class on "neat things" and "dull things" one might expect in each position and on how teamwork and cooperation are necessary.

Indicators of Success

- Students identify and describe the various jobs, demonstrating an increased awareness of the multiple roles necessary to bring a Broadway production to the stage and of the need for teamwork and cooperation for such an effort.

Follow-up

- Invite the director of a community theatre group to visit the class and talk about the various tasks involved in producing musicals. Have students prepare questions for the director based on their discussions of *Broadway Backstage!*
- Have students compare the production of a Broadway musical with the production of an opera.
- Have students follow similar steps in exploring the production of a symphony concert, a rock concert, a televised concert, a chamber music recital, and so on.

STANDARD 9A

Understanding music in relation to history and culture: Students classify by genre or style and by historical period or culture unfamiliar but representative aural examples of music and explain the reasoning behind their classifications.

Objective

- Students will describe similarities and differences in dance music from European Classical, contemporary American, and Native American cultures.

Materials

- Recordings of two current "popular" hits in different styles (for example, hip-hop and country western)

- Recording, with transcription, of "Shi Naasha," from *Music of the Sioux and the Navajo*, Ethnic Folkways Library RE 4401

- Recording of a minuet and trio by Wolfgang Amadeus Mozart

- Recording of Leonard Bernstein's "Jets," from *West Side Story*

- Audio-playback equipment

Prior Knowledge and Experiences

- Students have developed a basic music vocabulary.

- Students have developed critical listening skills.

- Students have had exposure to music from a variety of style periods and cultures.

Procedures

1. Play a thirty- to forty-five-second excerpts of recordings of current popular hits in different styles, asking students to describe or demonstrate dance steps for each.

2. Lead a brief discussion about why the dance steps would be different, including the following points: (a) differences in the music—tempo, rhythm patterns, timbre, articulation, and style; and (b) differences in origins or orientations of the music—for example, hip-hop originated in urban areas, country western in rural areas; people living in these different areas have different views of life.

3. Play twenty- to thirty-second excerpts of Bernstein's "Jets," the Navajo piece "Shi Naasha," and the Mozart minuet. Have students list words that describe timbre, rhythm, melody, harmony, and form (phrasing) in each.

4. Lead a discussion in which students compare their descriptions of the three pieces. Replay excerpts to verify elements described.

5. Have students speculate about the origin of each example, providing reasons for their guesses. Replay excerpts to reinforce points in the discussion, leading students to identification of European Classical, contemporary American, and Native American origins.

6. Point out that each of these compositions represents "dance music." Play each in its entirety, asking students to visualize dance movements that might be used with each.

Indicators of Success

- Students accurately describe elements of each excerpt and make reasoned associations with styles and cultures.

Follow-up

- Divide the class into three groups and have each group choreograph a dance for the twenty- to thirty-second excerpts used in steps 3–6.

- Select six to eight excerpts of music in styles similar to those used in steps 3–6. Record each on a separate tape. Have students, either individually or in small groups, classify each excerpt by culture or style period.

STANDARD 9C

Understaning music in relation to history and culture: Students identify various roles that musicians perform, cite representative individuals who have functioned in each role, and describe their activities and achievements.

Objective

- Students will identify and describe the various roles that musicians fulfill.

Materials

- Copies (for entire class) of students' reports on roles of musicians

Prior Knowledge and Experiences

- Students have listened to a broad range of musical styles and genres.

- Students have previously been assigned (and completed) two-to-three page research reports on two musicians (each of whom works in a different style), describing various roles they have fulfilled as musicians. Using library or Internet resources, they have developed lists of the accomplishments of each musician, classifying those accomplishments by roles such as composer, arranger, performer, conductor, critic, author, teacher, or recording technician.

Procedures

1. Have a student present his or her report and then distribute copies to the other students.

2. Have class ask questions of the presenter about the musicians, their roles, and their activities and accomplishments, and about the resources used for the report.

3. Then, ask the rest of the students to give their reports, pass out copies, and answer questions as the first student did.

4. Discuss with students the connections among the various roles of musicians and how those roles may vary depending on the style of music performed or the historical time period. Ask the class for examples from the reports they have heard.

5. Have students create a folder in which they will keep all the reports as their own reference source.

Indicators of Success

- Students identify the multiple roles of musicians and describe how these roles may differ according to the musical or historical context.

Follow-up

- Assign students to identify and interview musicians in the community, reporting to the class their findings regarding the various musical roles each fulfills within the community. Then invite local musicians to visit the class and discuss their respective roles as musicians.

Understanding music in relation to history and culture: Students identify and describe music genres or styles that show the influence of two or more cultural traditions, identify the cultural source of each influence, and trace the historical conditions that produced the synthesis of influences.

Objective

- Students will identify influences of Western popular and Native American music in a contemporary Native American piece.

Materials

- "Nihaa Shil Hozho," performed by XIT, listening lesson and recording from *Moving within the Circle: Contemporary Native American Music and Dance* by Bryan Burton (Danbury, CT: World Music Press, 1993), pages 110–12

- One other XIT recording—*Plight of the Redman, Relocation,* or *Silent Warrior* (Sound of America Records, PO Box 8606, Albuquerque, NM 87198; telephone 505-268-6110)

- Audio-playback equipment

- Paper

Prior Knowledge and Experiences

- Students have studied the style characteristics of Western popular music and of Native American music.

Procedures

1. Review the style characteristics of Western popular music and Native American music. Then explain to students that they will be hearing a recording of "Nihaa Shil Hozho" and that as they listen, they should list characteristics of Western and Native American styles that they hear in the music, including lyrics, melodic style, and use of particular instruments. Play the recording.

2. In a class discussion based on their lists, ask students to identify instruments as Western (guitar, strings, electric bass, synthesizer) or Native American (rattles, drums); to identify the melodic form as Western or Native American (Western AB form); and to identify the lyrics as Western or Native American (both: section A is in English; section B is in Navajo). Explain to students that terms of endearment and description in the song are drawn from Navajo poetic reference (for example, *hozho,* for "beauty").

3. Using the "Listening Experience" notes on pages 110–12 of *Moving within the Circle,* lead students in a discussion of how the two influences have become synthesized in contemporary Native American music. Have students give examples of specific Western performers who have influenced the style and of specific Native American musicians performing in the synthesized style.

4. Discuss with students the early influences of radio broadcasts reaching the reservations, of Western rock music on young Native Americans relocated to urban areas of the United States during the 1950s and 1960s, and of folk rock artist activists such as Bob Dylan and Joan Baez (sang about an awareness of social issues and calls for justice).

5. Play other recordings performed by XIT to reinforce the identification of the synthesis of Western popular and Native American music.

Indicators of Success

- Students identify stylistic elements of Western popular music and Native American music, instruments from Western and Native American cultures, and use of English and Navajo in lyrics of the contemporary Native American piece.

Follow-up

- Have students locate other examples of contemporary Native American music (for example, *Music for the Native Americans,* performed by Robbie Robertson and the Red Road Ensemble, Capitol Records CDP 7243 8 28295 2) and analyze them to determine influences of rock music.

Understanding music in relation to history and culture: Students identify and describe music genres or styles that show the influence of two or more cultural traditions, identify the cultural source of each influence, and trace the historical conditions that produced the synthesis of influences.

Objective

- Students will identify influences of Western popular and traditional Chinese music in current Chinese music.

Materials

- Computers with sound cards, speakers, and access to the World Wide Web

Prior Knowledge and Experiences

- Students have experience verbally describing music using technical vocabulary.

- Students have experience accessing the World Wide Web and downloading sound sources.

Procedures

1. Lead a brief discussion on the "shrinking of the world" and the intermixing of cultures. Stress the following points: (a) travel and communication enable people to move freely from one culture to another; (b) technology makes possible the exchange of cultural artifacts, foods, clothing, architecture, posters, visual art, and music; (c) exchange results in intermingling—for example, a painter may include visual images from several cultures on a single canvas, a composer may use rhythms from one culture, timbres from another, melodic lines from still another.

2. Introduce students to Web sites on Chinese music with foreign influence, such as: http://sunsite.unc.edu/pub/multimedia/chinese-music. For Chinese music with foreign influence, "click" Foreign Origin in the directory at that site; for Chinese urban music/modern popular music influenced by the West, click Modern Pops.

3. Have students, working in groups of two or three, download one of the following songs in the Foreign Origin section of the site: "Goodbye My Friend," "Lovely Light of Love," or "White Dove," or another appropriate song from the list that is given in that section. Ask them to listen to the song and list the features that are uniquely Chinese and those that are most likely a result of Western influence.

4. Have each group report to the class, playing excerpts of their chosen song and describing the aspects attributed to each culture.

Indicators of Success

- Students identify the rhythms and tonalities of the selected songs as being influenced by Western music and the timbres and texts as being traditional Chinese.

Follow-up

- Provide opportunities for students to hear and analyze music from other cultures. For example, Japanese, African, Latin American, and Native American music can be accessed at the student research page of the ARTSEDGE network: http://artsedge.kennedy-center.org/srp.html

RESOURCES

Sources of Songs Used in This Text

Campbell, Patricia Shehan, Ellen McCullough-Brabson, and Judith Cook Tucker. *Roots and Branches: A Legacy of Multicultural Music for Children.* Danbury CT: World Music Press, 1994. Accompanying recording.

Get America Singing . . . Again! Milwaukee: Hal Leonard Corporation, 1996.

Greatest American Song Book. Milwaukee: Hal Leonard Corporation, 1996.

I'll Be Seeing You: Fifty Songs of World War II. Milwaukee: Hal Leonard Corporation, 1995.

The Music Connection, Grades K–8. Parsippany, NJ: Silver Burdett Ginn, 1995.

Music and You, Grades K–8. New York: Macmillan/McGraw-Hill, 1991.

Novelty Song Book. Milwaukee: Hal Leonard Corporation, 1996.

Share the Music, Grades K–8. New York: Macmillan/McGraw-Hill, 1995.

TV Themes. Milwaukee: Hal Leonard Corporation, 1994.

Ware, Clifton. *Adventures in Singing.* New York: Glencoe/McGraw-Hill, 1995.

World of Music, Grades K–8. Parsippany, NJ: Silver Burdett Ginn, 1991.

Choral Music Used in This Text

"Betelehemu" by Wendell Whalum. New York: Lawson-Gould Music Publishers. SATB.

"Feller from Fortune," in *Elmer Iseler Choral Series,* arr. Harry Somers. Ft. Lauderdale, FL: Walton Music Corporation. SATB. Level 5.

"Gentle Annie" by Stephen Foster, arr. Dennis Elliot. Columbus, OH: Beckenhorst Press. SATB. Accompanying recording BP 113.

"Yonder Come Day," arr. Judith Cook Tucker. Danbury, CT: World Music Press. 2 or 3 parts.

Listening Selections Used in This Text

Bach, Johann Sebastian. Toccata in D minor.

Bartók, Béla. "Bagatelle," op. 6, no. 3.

Beethoven, Ludwig van. Symphony no. 6.

———. Symphony no. 9. Fourth movement.

Bernstein, Leonard. *West Side Story.*

Best of Kitaro. Kuckuck Music/Celestial Harmonies LC2099.

"Butterfly Dance." Native American music of the San Juan Pueblo Indians. Recording accompanying David Willoughby. *The World of Music,* 3rd ed. Madison, WI: Brown & Benchmark Publishers, 1996.

Copland, Aaron. *Rodeo.*

Creation's Journey. Smithsonian Folkways SF 40410.

Gagaku: Imperial Court Music of Japan. Lyrichord LLST 7126.

Gershwin, George. "An American in Paris."

Holst, Gustav. Suite in E♭ for Band. First movement.

Mozart, Wolfgang Amadeus. *Eine kleine Nachtmusik.* Rondo (fourth movement).

———. "Tuba Mirum," from *Requiem.*

Music for the Native Americans. Robbie Robertson and the Red Road Ensemble. Capitol Records CDP 7243 8 28295 2.

Music of the Sioux and the Navajo. Ethnic Folkways Library RE 4401.

1988 Billboard Top Hits. Rhino Records R2-7164.

Nylon Curtain. Billy Joel. Columbia 38200.

Out of Silence. Yanni. Private Music/BMG Publishing 2024-2-P.

Plight of the Redman. XIT. Sound of America Records, PO Box 8606, Albuquerque, NM 87198; telephone 505-268-6110.

Prokofiev, Sergey. *Peter and the Wolf.*

Red Thunder. Performed by Red Thunder. Canyon Records and Indian Arts, 4143 North 16th Avenue, Phoenix, AZ 85016.

Relocation. XIT. Sound of America Records, PO Box 8606, Albuquerque, NM 87198; telephone 505-268-6110.

Silent Warrior. XIT. Sound of America Records, PO Box 8606, Albuquerque, NM 87198; telephone 505-268-6110.

Smithsonian Collection of Classic Jazz, rev. ed. Selected and annotated by Martin Williams. Atlantic SD-310.

Sousa, John Philip. "Stars and Stripes Forever."

Spirituals in Concert. Kathleen Battle and Jesse Norman. Deutsche Grammophon 429790-2.

Verdi, Giuseppe. *La Traviata*, Act III, no. 16.

Vivaldi, Antonio. "Winter" (fourth movement), from *The Four Seasons*.

Wade in the Water: African American Sacred Music Traditions, with teacher's guide. Bernice Johnson Reagon, collector. Washington, DC: National Public Radio, 1994.

Webber, Andrew Lloyd. *The Phantom of the Opera*.

Williams, John. "The Imperial March," from *Star Wars*.

Other Materials Used in This Text

Aebersold, Jamey. *Major and Minor*, vol. 24 of *A New Approach to Jazz Improvisation*. Jamey Aebersold Jazz, PO Box 1244C, New Albany, IN 47151.

Alfred's Basic Guitar Method, Book 1. Van Nuys, CA: Alfred Publishing Company, 1959.

Bach, Johann Sebastian. *Clavierbüchlein for Anna Magdalena Bach*.

Band in a Box. Buffalo, NY: PG Music. Computer program.

Bartók, Béla. *The First Term at the Piano*. New York: Editio Musica Budapest/Boosey & Hawkes, 1929.

Bastien, James. *The Older Beginner Piano Course*, Level 1. San Diego: Neil A. Kjos Music Company, 1977.

Broadway Backstage! The Midtown Management Group, Inc., 120 West 44th Street, Suite 601, New York, NY 10036; telephone 212-398-6740. 1985. Videocassette.

Burakoff, Gerald, and Willy Strickland, arr. *Renaissance Time Pieces and Dances*. Fort Worth, TX: Sweet Pipes, 1983.

Burton, Bryan. *Moving within the Circle*. Danbury, CT: World Music Press, 1993. Accompanying recording.

Carley, Isabel McNeill. *For Hand Drums and Recorders*. Allison Park, PA: Music Innovations, 1982.

Finale.™ Eden Prairie, MN: Coda Music Technology. Computer program.

Fowler, Charles. *Music! Its Role and Importance in Our Lives*. New York: Glencoe/McGraw-Hill, 1994.

Lancaster, E. L., and Kenon D. Renfrow. *Group Piano for Adults*. Book 1, Van Nuys, CA: Alfred Publishing Company, 1995.

Lindeman, Carolynn A. *PianoLab: An Introduction to Class Piano*, 3rd ed.

Belmont, CA: Wadsworth Publishing Company, 1996.

Mozart, Wolfgang Amadeus. "Tuba Mirum," from *Requiem.* Score.

"My Savior's Love: Medley with 'And Can It Be' and 'I Stand Amazed in the Presence'," arr. Christine Anderson. Nashville: Word/Nelson Music.

Oates, Stephen B. *Let the Trumpet Sound: The Life of Martin Luther King, Jr.* New York: HarperCollins, 1994.

Reader's Digest Children's Songbook. Milwaukee: Hal Leonard Corporation, 1986.

Reel Music from Universal TV and Films. Milwaukee: Hal Leonard Corporation, 1985.

Schmid, Will. *Hal Leonard Guitar Method,* Book 1. Milwaukee: Hal Leonard Corporation, 1986.

Song Session Community Songbook. Miami: Warner Bros. Publications, 1995.

Telfer, Nancy. *Successful Warm-ups,* Book 1. San Diego: Neil A. Kjos Music Company, 1995.

Tolkien, J. R. R. *The Hobbit.* New York: Ballantine Books, 1937.

Vision. Palo Alto, CA: Opcode Systems. Computer program.

Winter, Robert. *Antonin Dvorak, Symphony #9.* New York: Voyager. CD-ROM program.

Wuytack, Jos. *Colores: Six Pièces pour Instruments à Percussion et Flûtes à bec.* Editions Musicales Alphonse Leduc, 175, rue Saint-Honoré, Paris.

Additional Resources

Allen, Jeffrey. *Guide to Karaoke Confidence.* Burbank, CA: Warner Bros. Publications, 1995.

*Anderson, William M., and Patricia Shehan Campbell. *Multicultural Perspectives in Music Education.* Reston, VA: Music Educators National Conference, 1996.

Bartholomew, John. *Steel Band.* New York: Oxford University Press, 1985.

Schmid, Will. *Something to Sing About.* Mission Hills, CA: Glencoe/McGraw-Hill, 1989.

Songs of the Civil War and Stephen Foster Favorites. Mormon Tabernacle Choir. Richard P. Condie. Sony Masterworks 48297.

* Available from MENC.

MENC Resources on Music and Arts Education Standards

Aiming for Excellence: The Impact of the Standards Movement on Music Education. 1996. #1012.

Implementing the Arts Education Standards. Set of five brochures: "What School Boards Can Do," "What School Administrators Can Do," "What State Education Agencies Can Do," "What Parents Can Do," "What the Arts Community Can Do." 1994. #4022. Each brochure is also available in packs of 20.

Music for a Sound Education: A Tool Kit for Implementing the Standards. 1994. #1600.

National Standards for Arts Education: What Every Young American Should Know and Be Able to Do in the Arts. 1994. #1605.

Opportunity-to-Learn Standards for Music Instruction: Grades PreK–12. 1994. #1619.

Performance Standards for Music: Strategies and Benchmarks for Assessing Progress Toward the National Standards, Grades PreK–12. 1996. #1633.

Perspectives on Implementation: Arts Education Standards for America's Students. 1994. #1622.

Prekindergarten Music Education Standards. Brochure. 1995. #4015 (set of 10).

The School Music Program—A New Vision: The K–12 National Standards, PreK Standards, and What They Mean to Music Educators. 1994. #1618.

Summary Statement: Education Reform, Standards, and the Arts. 1994. #4001 (pack of 10); #4001A (single copy).

Teaching Examples: Ideas for Music Educators. 1994. #1620.

The Vision for Arts Education in the 21st Century. 1994. #1617.

MENC's *Strategies for Teaching* Series

Strategies for Teaching Prekindergarten Music, compiled and edited by Wendy L. Sims. #1644.

Strategies for Teaching K–4 General Music, compiled and edited by Sandra L. Stauffer and Jennifer Davidson. #1645.

Strategies for Teaching Middle-Level General Music, compiled and edited by June M. Hinckley and Suzanne M. Shull. #1646.

Strategies for Teaching High School General Music, compiled and edited by Keith P. Thompson and Gloria J. Kiester. #1647.

Strategies for Teaching Elementary and Middle-Level Chorus, compiled and edited by Ann Roberts Small and Judy Bowers. #1648.

Strategies for Teaching High School Chorus, compiled and edited by Randal Swiggum. #1649.

Strategies for Teaching Strings and Orchestra, compiled and edited by Dorothy A. Straub, Louis S. Bergonzi, and Anne C. Witt. #1652.

Strategies for Teaching Middle-Level and High School Keyboard, compiled and edited by Martha F. Hilley and Tommie Pardue. #1655.

Strategies for Teaching Beginning and Intermediate Band, compiled and edited by Edward J. Kvet and Janet M. Tweed. #1650.

Strategies for Teaching High School Band, compiled and edited by Edward J. Kvet and John E. Williamson. #1651.

Strategies for Teaching Specialized Ensembles, compiled and edited by Robert A. Cutietta. #1653.

Strategies for Teaching Middle-Level and High School Guitar, compiled and edited by William E. Purse, James L. Jordan, and Nancy Marsters. #1654.

Strategies for Teaching: Guide for Music Methods Classes, compiled and edited by Louis O. Hall with Nancy R. Boone, John W. Grashel, and Rosemary C. Watkins. #1656.

For more information on these and other MENC publications, write to or call MENC Publications Sales, 1806 Robert Fulton Drive, Reston, VA 20191-4348; 800-828-0229.